DISCOVERING THE BIBLE

JONAH
and the
WHALE
and other Old Testament stories

RETOLD BY _Victoria Parker_

❖

CONSULTANT _Janet Dyson_

DISCOVERING THE BIBLE

JONAH
and the
WHALE
and other Old Testament stories

RETOLD BY _Victoria Parker_ ❖ CONSULTANT _Janet Dyson_

Published by Anness Publishing Ltd,
Blaby Road, Wigston, Leicestershire LE18 4SE

Email: info@anness.com

Web: www.annesspublishing.com

Anness Publishing has a new picture agency outlet for images for
publishing, promotions or advertising. Please visit our website
www.practicalpictures.com for more information.

Publisher: Joanna Lorenz
Managing Editor: Gilly Cameron Cooper
Senior Editor: Lisa Miles
Editorial Reader: Joy Wotton
Produced by Miles Kelly Publishing Limited
Publishing Director: Jim Miles
Editorial Director: Paula Borton
Art Director: Clare Sleven
Project Editor: Neil de Cort
Editorial Assistant: Simon Nevill
Designer: Jill Mumford
Information Author: Kamini Khanduri
Picture Research: Lesley Cartlidge and Libbe Mella,
Kate Miles and Janice Bracken
Copy Editing: AD Publishing Services
Indexing: Janet De Saulles
Design Consultant and Cover Design: Sarah Ponder
Education Consultant: Janet Dyson

ETHICAL TRADING POLICY
Because of our ongoing ecological investment programme, you, as our
customer, can have the pleasure and reassurance of knowing that a tree is
being cultivated on your behalf to naturally replace the materials used to
make the book you are holding. For further information about this
scheme, go to www.annesspublishing.com/trees

PUBLISHER'S NOTE
Although the advice and information in this book are believed to be
accurate and true at the time of going to press, neither the authors nor
the publisher can accept any legal responsibility or liability for any errors
or omissions that may have been made.

PHOTOGRAPHIC CREDITS
Page 6, (BL), Bryan Knox, Sonia Halliday Pictures.
Page 54 (BL), The Stock Market.
All other images from the Miles Kelly Archive
The Publishers would like to thank the following artists who have
contributed to this book:
Studio Galante (Virgil Pomfret Agency): L.R. Galante, Alessandro
Menchi, Manuela Cappon, Francesco Spadoni
Also: Sally Holmes, Rob Sheffield, Vanessa Card, Terry Riley, Peter Sarson,
Mark Bergin, Terry Gabbey (AFA), John James (Temple Rogers)
Maps by Martin Sanders

Contents

Introduction 6

Divided Kingdoms and Exile 8

King Ahab the Bad 10

Elijah's Challenge 12

The Still Small Voice 14

Ahab Strikes a Deal 16

Naboth's Vineyard 17

The Death of Ahab 18

Elijah's Chariot of Fire 20

Elisha and the Women 22

Naaman the Leper General 23

Saved from the Syrians 24

Jehu the Avenger 26

The End of Israel 28

Kings of Judah 30

Isaiah Shows the Way 32

King Hezekiah the Good 33

Josiah and the Law 34

Jeremiah's Warnings 36

The End of Judah 38

Ezekiel and the Exiles 40

Nebuchadnezzar's Dream 42

Belshazzar's Feast 44

Return from Exile 46

Rebuilding Jerusalem 48

Daniel and the Lions 50

Esther the Beautiful 52

Esther Saves the Jews 54

Jonah and the Whale 56

Old Testament Prophets 58

The Book of Psalms
Timeline 60

The Trials of Job 61

Glossary 62

Index 63

Introduction

THIS book tells of the rise and fall of the kingdoms of Israel and Judah, of the people who lived there and the kings who reigned over them. It describes the enemy empires – Syrian, Assyrian, Babylonian and Persian – that posed a constant threat to the Israelite nation. It also follows the lives of the prophets, from Elijah to Ezekiel, who struggled through these difficult times to sustain the Israelites' faith in God.

The two main prophets who lived in the kingdom of Israel were Elijah and Elisha. Elijah received his calling from God during the reign of King Ahab. Ahab had been persuaded by his wife, Jezebel, to join her in worshipping the Phoenician god, Baal. As more and more people followed the king and turned to Baal and other pagan gods, Elijah had his work cut out trying to turn them back to God.

Even after Elijah proved God's supremacy in a contest, Ahab continued to sin against God. When a man called Naboth refused to sell him his vineyard, the king had him stoned to death, then took the land. Elijah reminded him that, in refusing to sell his birthright, Naboth had been obeying God, and predicted that Ahab and his family would die in dishonour. His prediction came true, when Ahab was killed in battle, and his blood licked up by stray dogs.

Elijah is one of only two people in the Bible not to die – the other is Enoch, a man who enjoyed a particularly close fellowship with God. When the time came for Elijah to go to heaven, he was carried upwards in a flaming chariot. This amazing spectacle was witnessed by Elijah's assistant, Elisha. As Elisha picked up the cloak dropped by his master, the mantle of power passed to him.

Nebuchadnezzar's Palace
These are the remains of the palace of Nebuchadnezzar in Babylon. The exile was when the Israelites were forced from their homes in Judah to live in Babylon, but it is also the time when the Jewish faith was properly established.

Beth-shan, Israel
There were two important pagan temples here that stood at the time of the good King Josiah.

Elisha continued the work of Elijah, but when he failed to eliminate Baal worship God was forced to punish the Israelites. The mighty Assyrians besieged Israel's capital, Samaria, for three years and eventually took control of the city. The kingdom of Israel had come to an end, and its people were scattered throughout the vast Assyrian Empire.

Meanwhile, the smaller kingdom of Judah was facing the same problems. Despite the efforts of the prophet Isaiah, the people continued to worship pagan gods, and most kings didn't stop them. There were some exceptions – God rewarded the loyalty of King Hezekiah by stopping the Assyrians taking over Judah and giving the king an extra 15 years to live.

Then the Babylonians besieged Judah's capital, the holy city of Jerusalem, for two years. They destroyed the temple, burned the city to the ground and took most of the inhabitants to Babylon as exiles, ending the kingdom of Judah.

The exiled people of Judah became known to the Babylonians as Jews. A prophet called Ezekiel gradually managed to get the Jews to pull together and follow the laws of Moses in an attempt to preserve their own identity. They were rewarded by God and their lives began to improve. Ezekiel predicted that they would return to the Promised Land to rebuild their temple. This came true when the Babylonian King Cyrus eventually decided to allow the exiled Jews to return to Jerusalem. They rebuilt the temple and the city, and threw out all the non-Jews living there. God's people were back in the Promised Land. They had their temple and holy city and they were once again one nation under God.

The book ends with the stories of Daniel, the prophet who interpreted the dreams of kings and survived being thrown into a den of lions; Esther, the beautiful young wife of King Xerxes, who saved the Jews from destruction by appealing bravely to her husband; and Jonah, the unwilling prophet, who was swallowed by a whale as a punishment for disobeying the call of God.

The main thread running through this book is the lives and teachings of the prophets. The role of these people was to remind the Israelites of the covenant they had made with God during the time of Moses, and to warn them of the consequences of disobedience. Prophets were known as "men of God", but God often referred to them as His servants. The person usually held up as the best example of a prophet is Moses. All the features which characterized prophets were found in Moses. He received a specific and personal call from God. He was warned in advance of events and of their significance by God. He was concerned about the welfare of his people. He played an active role in the affairs of the nation. His prophesying was made up of a combination of proclaiming about the present situation and predicting the future.

God usually spoke to His prophets by simply making them aware of His message, but He also used dreams and visions. A prophet was often associated with a group of disciples, some of whom may have been called by God, while others joined the prophet to learn from his wisdom. It is most likely to have been these disciples who recorded the words of their masters in the books of the Bible.

From Egypt to the Promised Land

This book covers the lives of two of the greatest prophets, Elijah and Elisha, and tells the stories of the later kings of Israel and Judah.

THE LIFE OF ELIJAH
First Book of Kings, Ch. 17 to 22.
Second Book of Kings, Ch. 1 & 2.
THE LIFE OF ELISHA
Second Book of Kings, Ch. 3 to 17.
KINGS OF ISRAEL AND JUDAH
Second Book of Kings, Ch. 11 to 25.
THE PROPHETS
Isaiah Ch. 1 to 9.
Jeremiah Ch. 1 to 36.
THE EXILE
Jeremiah Ch. 40.
Ezekiel Ch. 18 to 37.
Daniel, Ch. 1 to 6.
THE RETURN FROM EXILE
Ezra, Ch. 1 to 10.
Haggai, Ch. 1.
Nehemiah, Ch. 1 to 6.
ESTHER
Esther, Ch. 3 to 8.
JONAH
Jonah, Ch. 1 to 4.

Jerusalem at the centre of the world
The picture on the right is an ancient map of what was known of the world at the time of Ptolemy, an Egyptian ruler who lived in AD 100. Even at this time Jerusalem, capital of Judah, was a very important city. This world map places Jerusalem at its centre.

Divided Kingdoms and Exile

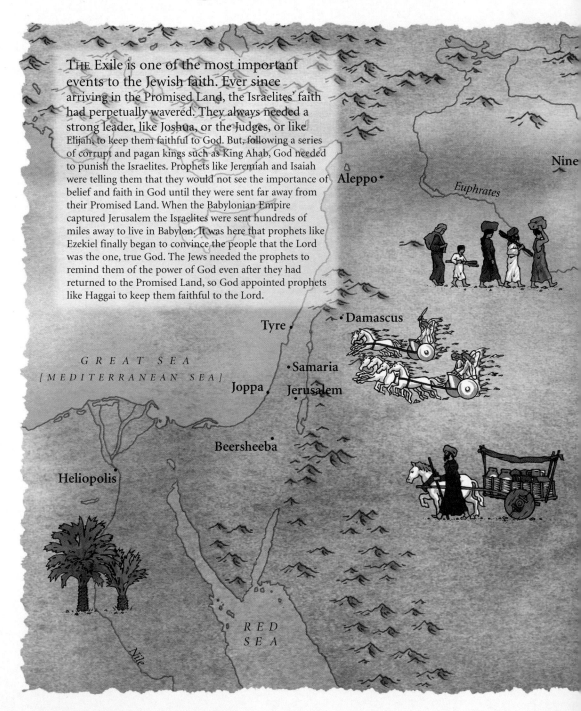

THE Exile is one of the most important events to the Jewish faith. Ever since arriving in the Promised Land, the Israelites' faith had perpetually wavered. They always needed a strong leader, like Joshua, or the Judges, or like Elijah, to keep them faithful to God. But, following a series of corrupt and pagan kings such as King Ahab, God needed to punish the Israelites. Prophets like Jeremiah and Isaiah were telling them that they would not see the importance of belief and faith in God until they were sent far away from their Promised Land. When the Babylonian Empire captured Jerusalem the Israelites were sent hundreds of miles away to live in Babylon. It was here that prophets like Ezekiel finally began to convince the people that the Lord was the one, true God. The Jews needed the prophets to remind them of the power of God even after they had returned to the Promised Land, so God appointed prophets like Haggai to keep them faithful to the Lord.

Nine

Aleppo

Euphrates

Tyre

Damascus

GREAT SEA
[MEDITERRANEAN SEA]

Samaria

Joppa

Jerusalem

Beersheeba

Heliopolis

RED
SEA

Nile

HYRCANIAN
SEA

sshur

Tigris

• Babylon
    • Nippur

LOWER
SEA

Persepolis

King Ahab the Bad

AFTER the reign of King Solomon, the Promised Land split into two kingdoms. The ten northern tribes kept the Promised Land's name – Israel. The smaller kingdom of Judah, formed by the two southern tribes, kept the capital, Jerusalem, and the temple built by King Solomon.

King Jeroboam of Israel was worried. He knew that his ten tribes would want to travel to the temple at certain times, as was the custom. And if his subjects felt that God's home was in Judah, wouldn't they eventually want to be ruled by the king of Judah instead? Jeroboam decided to set up two massive altars in his own country, at

Bethel and Dan, with a huge golden statue of a calf for each one. He appointed his own priests, with new prayer services and feast days. Then he appointed a new capital city for Israel, Samaria.

But in fact King Jeroboam need not have worried. The Hebrews in Judah were deserting the temple in droves and taking up pagan religions, which seemed to be much more fun. At pagan festivals the people ate and drank what they wanted, and danced with who they wanted – their gods didn't seem to mind at all. So statues of idols began to pop up all over Judah and their king did nothing to stop it.

For years, evil king followed evil king in both kingdoms. But Ahab, the sixth king of Israel, was one of the very worst. Ahab married Jezebel, the daughter of the king of Sidon, who worshipped the pagan god Baal. Jezebel persuaded Ahab to worship Baal too, and soon nearly all the Hebrews in Israel were worshipping Baal at a huge temple that Ahab built in Samaria.

> " *And Ahab did evil in the sight of the Lord more than all that were before him.* "

But not everyone abandoned God. The Lord called a faithful man named Elijah to take a message to King Ahab: "I am the God of Israel, whom you have forgotten. There will be no rain in the country until I say so."

The king just laughed. But before long, the weather got drier and drier. Ahab got angrier and angrier, and the Lord told Elijah to hide. Elijah headed east, as God instructed,

Jezebel
Jezebel was a Phoenician princess, married to King Ahab of Israel. When she arrived in Samaria, she continued to worship her native god, Baal. Jezebel encouraged her husband, his court and the whole of Israel to turn away from their God towards Baal. Ten years after Ahab died, Jezebel came to a violent end – she was thrown from the window of her palace by her servants, under the orders of King Jehu.

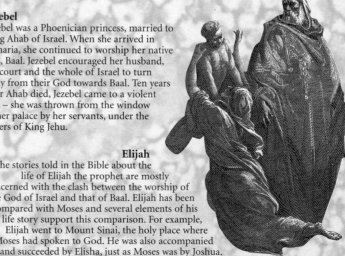

Elijah
The stories told in the Bible about the life of Elijah the prophet are mostly concerned with the clash between the worship of the God of Israel and that of Baal. Elijah has been compared with Moses and several elements of his life story support this comparison. For example, Elijah went to Mount Sinai, the holy place where Moses had spoken to God. He was also accompanied and succeeded by Elisha, just as Moses was by Joshua.

next day... and the next day... in fact, every day that Elijah was there. But despite the plentiful food, her son fell sick with a fever and, after several days, died.

"You say you're a man of God," she cried to Elijah. "Have I done anything wrong to deserve my son's death?" The prophet took the lifeless body to his own bed. He laid the boy down and knelt beside him. Three times Elijah cried out to God to give back the child's soul, and three times he listened for the child's heart to start beating again.

Soon, when Elijah carried the boy downstairs to his mother, he was alive.

until he reached the brook of Cherith. There, Elijah found a cave for shelter. The drought was so bad that there wasn't an animal or a blade of grass in sight. But the Lord didn't let Elijah go hungry. Morning and evening ravens arrived at the cave carrying meat and bread for him in their beaks. Then the brook dried up in the sweltering sun. "Go to Zarephath," came the Lord's voice. "There's a widow there who will look after you."

Sure enough, Elijah was taken in by a very poor widow who had only a handful of flour and a little oil left for herself and her son to eat. Nevertheless, she made Elijah a meal and resigned herself to starving to death. Yet the next day she was amazed to find that her flour jar and oil jug were full once again... and the

God the provider
This picture shows Elijah being fed by ravens. God demonstrates His superiority as He is able to provide for Elijah even in the heartland of Baal worship.

Samarian ivory
The building of Samaria was begun by King Omri and continued by his son, Ahab. This piece of ivory from the palace dates from the 9th century BC and shows the Egyptian god Horus.

❖ **ABOUT THE STORY** ❖

The reason why the people preferred Baal to the true God was that worshipping him was much easier and less demanding. However, the story of Elijah reminds readers that God always keeps a few people faithful to Himself and uses them to challenge others to return to Him. Believers may be few in number at times , but they are all very important to God's purposes.

Elijah's Challenge

As God had commanded there had been no rain for three years. Elijah heard God telling him to go and find the furious King Ahab before Ahab found him. The king hated to obey Elijah, but he followed all his instructions: he needed the rain. He summoned the 450 priests of Baal and also the 400 priests of Asherah (Jezebel's other god) and ordered all his subjects to go to Mount Carmel.

The prophet was waiting for them. "The Lord God has brought this terrible drought upon Israel because you are sinning against Him and worshipping idols," Elijah told the king, sternly. "Let's settle this once and for all. I challenge your priests to a contest. Tell them to prepare a bull for sacrifice to their gods and I'll prepare another for sacrifice to the Lord. But no one must set either offering alight.

We'll all pray to our gods to miraculously light the fire themselves. And whoever has their prayer answered will obviously be worshipping the true god."

When everything was in place, Ahab and Jezebel's priests began to call upon Baal to light the offering. All morning they prayed, chanting themselves into a trance and dancing themselves mad. In their frenzy, they even slashed themselves with their sacrificial knives. But it was no use. Not a spark, not even a puff of smoke.

> 66 *They raved on but there was no voice; no one answered, no one heeded.* 99

Mount Carmel
This is a view down Mount Carmel, which is also the name given to a group of mountains in north-west Israel. It is believed to be the site of Elijah's contest with the prophets of Baal. In Bible times, it was covered in oak and olive groves.

Jezebel's seal
This picture shows a seal from the 9th-8th centuries BC. The name 'Jezebel' has been added in Phoenician letters. Jezebel was a Phoenician princess.

Elijah enjoyed watching the priests make fools of themselves. "Shout louder," he mocked. "Maybe your god is having a nap!" At midday the priests of Baal and Asherah gave up, exhausted. It was Elijah's turn. First Elijah took 12 large stones, one for each of the tribes of the Promised Land, and he rebuilt the altar to the Lord that had once stood at the top of Mount Carmel. He arranged the firewood and laid his bull on it, then he dug a deep trench all around. Elijah ordered the Israelites to fetch water and pour it over the altar. The astonished Israelites drenched the animal and the wood until the water filled the trench.

Then Elijah stood before the altar and prayed. The thousands of waiting men and women fell silent. "Lord, show these people that you are the one true God, and that I am your servant and have done everything at your command," the prophet called aloud. There was a mighty roar as the sodden heap burst into flame, and everything was burnt to ashes: not just the bull and the firewood, but the stones and the soil too! The terrified crowds were beaten back by the immense heat and fell to the ground to worship the one true God. Elijah pointed at the trembling priests of Baal and Asherah. "Kill them," he ordered. "Make sure not one of them escapes, for they have led you all into sin." At once the Israelites fell on the evil men.

King Ahab was enraged. But the prophet simply ordered him to calm down and have a meal.

Meanwhile, Elijah prayed while his servant watched the sky for rain. Suddenly Elijah's servant shouted out. "A little cloud as small as a man's hand is heading this way!"

"It is the rain," smiled Elijah. "Quick, Ahab! Get in your chariot and drive home before the storm overtakes you!" The king raced down the mountain as black thunder clouds chased him all the way to his royal city of Jezreel. As for Elijah, he was filled with the spirit of the Lord, and ran so fast that he beat the king back to the palace.

Fire from God
The illustration shows Elijah's sacrifice bursting into flames, while the prophet himself prays beside it. The sacrifice of the priests of Baal was not set alight.

Fleeing from the storm
In this picture, Ahab and Elijah are shown fleeing from the storm. Because the spirit of God came upon Elijah, he was able to run very fast and reached Jezreel before Ahab.

The Still Small Voice

WHEN King Ahab told Jezebel about Elijah's show of power on Mount Carmel, the queen turned purple. She shook with rage. She spat, she spluttered and finally exploded. "Find that trouble-making prophet!" she screamed at a messenger. "Tell him that by tomorrow he'll be in exactly the same place as my dead priests!"

In fear for his life, Elijah fled; first south into the kingdom of Judah and then into the desert. How depressed and worn out he was! All his efforts before the people at Mount Carmel had not been enough. He'd failed to turn the king and queen back to the Lord, and the Israelites would soon be back to worshipping their pagan idols once again. The prophet didn't have the will to go on any longer. He sank down under a broom tree. "Lord, I've had enough," he groaned. "Let me die right here." Exhausted, he fell into a deep, troubled sleep.

The touch of a gentle hand brought Elijah back to consciousness. Through his bleary eyes, he saw that the hand belonged to an angel, and at once the prophet was wide awake. "Get up now," the angel said, kindly. "You must be hungry." Elijah turned to look where the angel indicated and saw that a jug of fresh water stood next to some freshly baked loaves of bread. The smell was irresistible, and Elijah gratefully tucked in. With his stomach full and his mind much comforted, the prophet drifted off once more. But this time his dreams were easy. And when he awoke, the angel was there again. "Come and eat," came the soft voice, "or you won't be fit to make the journey." The journey that the angel wanted

Elijah to make was a long one – 40 days and 40 nights through the desert. But the special food and drink had revived Elijah more than he would ever have imagined, and he made it safely to Mount Horeb, the holy place where Moses himself had spoken to God. It was the perfect place to hide and wait for the Lord's instructions.

> " *And behold, a voice said, 'What are you doing here, Elijah?'* "

Day after day Elijah sat inside a cave and wondered what would happen next. The prophet had totally lost track of time when he heard the Lord's voice calling him. It took him completely by surprise. "Elijah! Elijah!" God said. "What are you doing here?"

The prophet leapt to his feet and spoke aloud into the darkness. "Of all the people in Israel, only I remain faithful to you, Lord," Elijah called. "Because of this, they want to kill me."

"Go from this cave and stand outside on the mountain," God ordered.

Elijah had hardly stuck his nose out into the

open when the wind began to blow. First, a brisk breeze lifted the fallen leaves and swirled them around; then the wind howled into a gale that plucked trees out of the ground and ripped rocks from the mountainside and tossed them around like pebbles. And Elijah stood safe and unafraid with the hurricane roaring round him. He did not feel that God was in the wind.

Next, the ground underneath the prophet began to tremble... then to shake... then to shudder... and with a mighty crack, the mountain split in two. Elijah stood safe and unafraid on the heaving soil. He did not feel that God was in the earthquake.

All at once there was a blaze of flame and a rush of heat as every tree, plant and blade of grass caught fire. Elijah stood safe and unafraid while the flames licked all around him. He did not feel that God was in the inferno either.

Finally, the wind dropped, the earth juddered to a halt and the flames died away. Elijah was left alone in the silence of the mountainside. Then he heard a still, small voice speaking quite clearly into his mind – and he felt the Lord was there. Deeply afraid, he hid his face in his cloak and listened. "Go to Damascus in Syria and find two men: Hazael and Jehu. Anoint them as future kings: Hazael, king of Syria, and Jehu, king of Israel. They will wreak terrible destruction on King Ahab and his sinning subjects, and I will be avenged by them for the wrongs the Israelites have done me. When you have finished in Syria, go and find Elisha, the son of Shaphat. He is to be your assistant and will take over from you when your work for me is done. And do not be discouraged. There remain 7,000 people in Israel who have not worshipped Baal and who are true to me."

Elijah set off for Syria with renewed energy and hope. No matter how gloomy things looked, God had shown him that He was always there and would deal with things in His own good time. And with Elisha for a companion, Elijah would no longer have to face the sinning Israelite nation on his own.

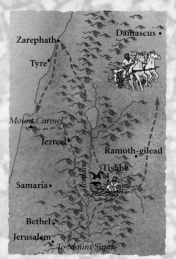

ELIJAH WAS UPSET WHEN HIS LIFE WAS THREATENED. HE PANICKED AND RAN AWAY. HE WAS VERY TIRED. PEOPLE MAKE BAD DECISIONS WHEN THEY ARE TIRED. WHAT THEY NEED TO DO IS STOP AND PRAY.

The journey of Elijah
Elijah travelled all over Israel to follow God's commands. He first heard God speak to him in Tishbe, and had his competition with the Baal prophets after going to Zarephath. He then fled to Mount Sinai, before going up to heaven on the chariot of fire.

❖ ABOUT THE STORY ❖

Elijah was used to seeing God act in spectacular ways. Wind represented His powerful Spirit, the earthquake was a sign of His judgement and fire was what He had spoken through on Mount Carmel. Elijah had to learn that God works in many different, quieter, ways too. God had quietly kept other people faithful to Himself, but Elijah had been too busy to notice.

Ahab Strikes a Deal

WHEN Ahab was king of Israel, the strongest nation in the region was Syria, under King Benhadad. Benhadad wanted to take Ahab's kingdom for himself. He gathered together his armies, marched into Israel, and soon reached Samaria. King Ahab's capital city was besieged; thousands of soldiers were ready to attack.

Ahab despaired. But a prophet arrived with a message from the Lord. "I will give these enemies into your hands. By this, you will know that I am the one true God. Send the servants of your district governors out to fight."

The king was mystified, but armed the 232 servants and pushed the shocked men outside the city walls to face the full might of the Syrian army.

Ahab couldn't believe his eyes. The servants hacked their way through the enemy lines. He sent reinforcements and soon Benhadad's men were either dead or scattered.

Ahab was overjoyed, but the prophet warned him that Benhadad had escaped and that Syria would attack again. Sure enough, in the spring, the Syrians appeared again. Once more the prophet told Ahab: "The Lord will again give you victory to prove He is the one true God."

By sunset, the smaller army of Israel had slain 100,000 Syrians. The stunned invaders tried to flee to the city of Aphek, but in the jostle to get through the gates the city wall collapsed, crushing many to death. King Benhadad was one of the lucky few who made it through. To try and escape with his life, the defeated king offered to return all the Israelite cities he had conquered, and let the Israelites trade with Syria. Ahab accepted, and the deal was sealed.

The Israelite king was triumphant, but a prophet gave him a grave message. "The Lord is angry with you for sparing this enemy," he said. "God will take your life instead of his, and your people instead of his." Ahab's heart sank, and he resented the word of the Lord.

✦ ABOUT THE STORY ✦

Nothing seems to be enough to convince Ahab that the Lord is all-powerful. Unconvinced by the contest on Mount Carmel, the Lord shows Ahab his power by helping him win two great victories against armies that were better trained and far outnumbered his own. Rather than humiliating Ahab in front of his own people the Lord helps him, but the king still does not accept the word of the Lord and remains completely unrepentant.

Syrian prince
This statue from around 800BC shows a Syrian prince, seated on a throne, with his feet on a footstool. He is armed with a dagger and wears a necklace with symbols of the sun and moon. It is possible that King Benhadad might have looked like this.

Trading places
In return for saving Benhadad's life, Ahab was allowed to set up trading places in Damascus. The jewellery being bought and sold there might have looked like these necklaces, made of gold, lapis lazuli and cornelian.

Naboth's Vineyard

IN Samaria, next door to King Ahab's palace, there was a beautiful vineyard which belonged to a man called Naboth. Every day the king would look out of his window and dream of the wonderful fruits and vegetables he would grow for himself if only he owned the fertile earth.

One day a royal messenger knocked on Naboth's door. "The king wants your vineyard," he said bluntly. "You can either swap it for any vineyard you want or the king will pay you good money for it."

Naboth pondered for a moment. "This land has belonged to my family for generations," he thought. "I wouldn't part with it for any sum of money, and besides, the Lord says that it's a sin to sell someone your birthright." Naboth looked at the messenger. "Tell the king he can't have my vineyard," he said firmly. "It's God's law that I can't part with it."

The king was extremely annoyed. He lay in his bedroom in a mood, refusing to eat anything. "Cheer up!" Jezebel laughed. "I'll get you the vineyard." The wicked queen wrote a letter to each of the elders in the city. She forged Ahab's name and sealed each letter with the king's royal seal. The plot was set.

Some weeks later there was a great ceremony in the public square. As Naboth stood on the platform in front of all the citizens, two men began to lie that they had heard him curse both God and the king. "Treason! Treason!" cried the corrupt elders and nobles, stirring up the crowd into a frenzy. And the innocent, bewildered Naboth was dragged outside the city and stoned to death.

The delighted king trotted off to claim the vineyard. However, as he strutted round it the prophet Elijah came striding up to him. "The price you have paid for this vineyard is your very soul," the furious prophet thundered. "Because of your crimes against the Lord, you and all of your family will be wiped out. The dogs will lick up your blood and the birds will peck at your bones."

> ‟ *'Where dogs licked up the blood of Naboth shall dogs lick your blood.'* ”

Ahab was terrified at the words of the great prophet. He wept and tore his clothes. He put on sackcloth and fasted, all to try and earn some mercy from God. When the Lord saw that Ahab was at last taking some notice of Him, He promised to show him a little mercy, but as for complete forgiveness – it was far too late for that.

Breaking the law
According to God's law, it was forbidden to sell land that had been inherited from one's ancestors. The picture above shows Ahab and Naboth in the vineyard.

Ahab's seal
This is a picture of Ahab's seal. It is a bronze ring and the inscription on it reads "Ahab, king of Israel". Jezebel would have used this seal to forge Ahab's signature on the letters she wrote.

❖ **ABOUT THE STORY** ❖

Ahab knew that the law said he couldn't take Naboth's vineyard. But Jezebel, who cared nothing for God's law, believed the king could do anything. But she knew that simply taking the vineyard would cause a riot, so she lied and murdered to get it. The Bible has many stories about people who misused their power, and shows that God's law is to be obeyed by everyone, however famous, rich or powerful they are.

The Death of Ahab

IT didn't take long for Elijah's prophecies of disaster to start striking the royal family. And it was King Ahab himself who met his doom first. The king of Israel had become friendly with his rival, King Jehoshaphat of Judah. Ahab suggested that he and Jehoshaphat should together attack Syria to win back the city of Ramoth-gilead, which was in the hands of King Benhadad. "What do you think?" Ahab asked the king of Judah. "You can consider my forces your own," Jehoshaphat assured him. "Only let's first consult the Lord about this plan."

King Ahab called all the prophets in Israel to the palace. "We want to know whether we should fight the Syrians for Ramoth-gilead," King Ahab said. The prophets all agreed. "The Lord says yes..." said some. "The Lord will give you victory..." urged yet more. One of them, Zedekiah, even approached the thrones wearing a horned battle helmet! But for some reason, Ahab felt uneasy about the prophets' enthusiasm. He looked around the room. Someone was missing.

"Where's Micaiah?" the king said slowly. "Bring him here at once." Ahab explained why to Jehoshaphat. "Micaiah is a troublesome prophet," he sighed. "He never tells me what I want to hear. But because of this, I tend to believe him more than the rest. They just seem to agree with everything I say."

When Micaiah arrived, he at first went along with the other prophets.

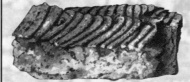
Preserved armour
This coat of mail found at Nuzi, in Iraq, dates from around 1400BC and is made of overlapping bronze scales. This is the sort of armour Ahab would have worn.

Coat of mail
Coats of mail were worn by archers who were unable to protect themselves with shields. They were more protective than leather armour and lighter than plate armour. Their weak point was the joints of the sleeves, which is probably where the arrow that killed Ahab entered.

"Go and triumph," he told the king, "God will grant you victory." But Ahab looked him in the eye.

"Come now, Micaiah," he insisted. "Tell me the truth."

Just as Ahab feared, Micaiah then prophesied doom and gloom. "I have seen all Israel scattered upon the mountains like sheep with no shepherd," he began.

Ahab groaned and turned to Jehoshaphat. "You see, I told you so. He never has a good word to say for me."

Micaiah continued, "I saw the Lord in heaven, wondering how He could persuade you to attack the Syrians. One of the angels said He'd put lies in the mouths of your prophets so they'd advise you to go to battle."

Zedekiah flew into a fury. He struck Micaiah across the face. "How dare you say that God lies to us and yet speaks truthfully through you?"

"You'll see that I'm right on the day that you run and hide in the face of defeat," Micaiah answered.

At the mention of the word "defeat", King Ahab decided he'd listened to quite enough. "Arrest this man!" he cried to his guards. "Keep him in prison on bread and water until I return victorious and decide what to do with him."

Micaiah remained completely unruffled. "If you return victorious, my name's not Micaiah," he said calmly.

Despite the Israelite king's outward show of confidence, he was inwardly very worried by Micaiah's words. Ahab let Jehoshaphat go into battle dressed in his king's robes and riding in his royal chariot, while he disguised himself as an ordinary soldier. Benhadad of Syria had ordered his chariot regiment to attack no one but the king of Israel, and they nearly killed Jehoshaphat by mistake, thinking that he was Ahab.

However, one of Benhadad's archers, firing at random, delivered the king of Israel's mortal wound. An arrow pierced a chink between the plates of metal and embedded itself deep in his flesh. A faithful horseman carried the wounded king out of the fighting, and all day he lay in his chariot, watching his troops being slaughtered. After sweltering and bleeding all day in the hot sun, that evening King Ahab died and his troops disbanded and fled.

> " *They washed the chariot by the pool of Samaria, and the dogs licked up his blood.* "

Ahab's body was taken home to Samaria and buried there. But it was at a spot near to where Naboth had been stoned to death that his chariot was washed clean. And as Ahab's blood streamed out of the chariot floor, stray dogs came and licked it up, just as Elijah had said they would.

Micaiah
Micaiah was a prophet during Ahab's reign. Apart from this story of his meeting with the king, little else is known about him. He may have been brought out of prison to prophesy in this case. He had obviously prophesied regularly before as Ahab was already aware of his gloomy, but truthful and accurate, predictions.

Cleaning the chariot
The above picture shows people cleaning out Ahab's chariot after his death. The blood is being licked up by stray dogs, fulfilling Elijah's prophecy.

Elijah's Chariot of Fire

ELIJAH sighed. He had to go on a journey, and he knew it would be his last. "God is sending me to Bethel," he told his assistant, Elisha. "Don't come with me. I won't need you this time." But Elisha sensed what lay behind his master's words and he insisted on keeping Elijah company.

When the two companions reached the far-off town, Elisha found out that he wasn't the only one who knew what was about to happen. The prophets living at Bethel whispered to him worriedly. "Do you know that the Lord is going to take Elijah from us?" they gasped.

"Yes, I know," Elisha reassured them. "Keep it to yourselves." And he hurried back to his master.

"Why don't you stay here, Elisha?" the older prophet urged. "The Lord has told me that I've got to go further on, to Jericho."

"You're not getting rid of me that easily," smiled the young man, striding out determinedly.

They drew near to Jericho and saw the prophets of the city waiting for them. Once again, Elisha was beckoned aside. "The Lord is going to..." they began.

"Hush, now," interrupted Elisha. "I know. Now try to keep it quiet." And he dashed back to his master.

"Honestly, Elisha," insisted the older prophet, "I really think you should stay here. God now says that I've got to go all the way to the River Jordan."

"As long as the Lord's above and you're alive down here, I'll never leave you," said the faithful young man. And the companions went on down the road, followed by a group of about 50 prophets, who hung back nervously.

Elijah and Elisha reached the Jordan. Elijah took off his cloak, rolled it up and struck the waters with it. The river parted, leaving a dry path. The two men crossed without even getting their feet wet.

Then Elijah turned to Elisha and smiled sadly. "You know that I'm going to be taken from you," he said. "Is there anything you'd like to ask me or do for you?"

"Master," Elijah said, "I need a double share of your spirit in order to do your job."

Crossing the Jordan
The crossing of the River Jordan that Elijah and Elisha made reminds us of the miracle that Moses performed when he parted the waves of the Red Sea. When Elisha also performed the same miracle, it showed that he had indeed taken over from Elijah.

✤ ABOUT THE STORY ✤
This great vision was God's way of telling Elisha that he was called to a very special job, carrying on the work that Elijah had started. Elijah wasn't able to promise the "double share" of his power, because only God could give that, but he believed God would answer Elisha's prayer. There was nothing magical about Elijah's cloak, but it is symbolic of the fact that Elisha is taking over Elijah's role.

Elijah shook his head. "That's something I can't promise to give you," he replied. "However, if God allows you to see me taken up to heaven then I'm sure He will give you what you ask."

Elisha saw everything. It started as a glimmer in the sky that swirled and glowed until it became a flaming chariot drawn by horses of fire that landed between them. Elisha watched in awe as Elijah got in and raised one hand in farewell. Then the horses began to gallop in circles until everything was a blazing whirlwind. The chariot rushed upwards and was gone.

> **Behold, a chariot of fire and horses of fire separated the two of them.**

Elisha knew that he'd never see his master again and began to mourn. Then he noticed Elijah's cloak lying on the ground. Rolling up the cloak, he cried aloud, "Where is the God of Elijah?" He struck the waters of the River Jordan and once more the river parted to let him through.

When the 50 prophets saw Elisha's miracle, they knew that the spirit of Elijah had come on him, and they bowed down before him. But they found it hard to accept that the great prophet was really gone. "May we go and look for Elijah?" they begged. Elisha was reluctant to let them go, but realised they hadn't seen what he had seen.

After three days of searching, the prophets returned. They knew in their hearts that Elijah was in heaven and wouldn't be coming back.

A first-born son
Elisha is not being greedy or arrogant when he asks Elijah for a "double share". A first-born son usually inherited a double portion of a parent's estate, so it is more that Elisha wants to be recognised as Elijah's spiritual heir.

Elisha, Elijah and the prophets
The Bible tells us that a group of prophets followed Elijah and Elisha round the country. The "prophets" in this case are not the same as Elijah and Elisha. They are people who try to live good lives, but God does not speak directly to them.

Elisha and the Women

ELISHA travelled and spread the word of God, working many miracles that established his reputation as a great prophet.

In Jericho, he purified the foul-tasting water that gushed from the city's main spring.

Elisha also helped a woman so poor that she had only a single jar of oil. She was deep in debt, and her creditor was about to take her children into slavery as settlement. Elisha told her to borrow empty jars and begin pouring her own oil into them. To her astonishment, as long as there were jars to be filled, the oil kept flowing. She had more than enough oil to sell to pay off her debts.

In Shunem, a rich woman made Elisha and his servant, Gehazi, welcome in her house. The prophet wondered how he could repay her kindness. Then Gehazi mentioned that the wealthy couple didn't have a child. "This time next year, you will have a son," Elisha told them. And to the couple's great joy, they did.

Some years later, Elisha was praying at Mount Carmel with Gehazi when the woman came hurrying up, weeping her heart out. "My son is dead!" she sobbed. "He was brought home this morning with a bad headache and by lunchtime he was lifeless in my arms! You're a holy man, please do something!" At once, Elisha hurried to the woman's home.

> *As he stretched himself upon him, the flesh of the child became warm.*

When they got there, Elisha quietly shut the door to the dead child's room and prayed. Then he stretched his hands out over the small, stiff body. Elisha sensed his skin gradually warming up and felt gentle breath on his face. "A-choo!" the child sneezed. "A-choo! A-choo!" God had answered the great prophet's prayers to bring the dead boy back to life.

Oil jar
The Bible refers to the use of oil a great deal, and it usually refers to olive oil. Oil was used for cooking as much in Elisha's time at it is now, but it was also an offering to God, used for trade and as fuel for lamps.

MIRACULOUS STORIES OF PROPHETS HEALING THE FAITHFUL REMIND US THAT GOD PROTECTS HIS PEOPLE. THESE STORIES ENCOURAGE FAITH WHEN TIMES ARE HARD.

The widow's oil
This is an illustration of the story based on a picture in a 13th-century Spanish Bible. Many Bibles throughout history have been very lavishly illustrated, not only with pictures but with decorated letters.

Naaman the Leper General

WHEN the Syrians took some of the Israelites captive, they heard the amazing stories of Elisha. The general of the Syrian army, Naaman, was particularly interested. He had leprosy, a terrible skin disease. His wife's Israelite maid was sure that Elisha would be able to cure him, so Naaman asked the king if he could go to find the prophet.

> " *He was a mighty man of valour, but he was a leper.* "

When Naaman and his royal entourage arrived at Elisha's house, Naaman was annoyed to find that the prophet wouldn't come out but sent a servant instead. "Elisha says to tell you to bathe seven times in the River Jordan," Gehazi said. "Goodbye." And he shut the door.

Naaman was furious. He'd come all this way to see the holy man, and he'd brought magnificent gifts, too: sacks of silver, bags of gold and ten very expensive robes. "All Elisha had to do was pray a bit!" he raged. "If it's just a matter of washing, we've got better rivers back at home!" Humiliated, he was about to head straight back to Syria, when one of his attendants stopped him.

"Sir, you've nothing to lose," he said. "You've come all the way here, and it's an easy thing to do. Why not try?"

Once... twice... three times Naaman washed himself in the Jordan. The sores were there just the same. Four... five... six – nothing. But as he rose from the waters for the seventh time, he knew something was different. He looked down and saw that his skin was as smooth as a child's.

Naaman jumped for joy, then ran to thank Elisha. "Now I know that your God is the true God," he said. "May I take some earth to worship him when I return home?"

"Of course," said the delighted prophet, but he wouldn't accept a single gift that Naaman tried to press upon him.

When Naaman had left, Elisha noticed that Gehazi was missing. Instantly, he knew his servant had gone to tell Naaman that his master had changed his mind about the gifts, so he could take them for himself.

When Gehazi returned the prophet knew what he had done and was unforgiving. "Now you have Naaman's wealth, you can have his leprosy too," Elisha thundered, and the horrified servant felt his skin begin to bubble.

Aramean architecture
The Syrians were known at this time as "Arameans", and Syria was called "Aram." The picture shows the base of a column from an Aramean palace. The sphinx is a mythical animal that is seen in art and architecture all over the world. Solomon had sphinxes, called cherubim in Israel, in the temple he built at Jerusalem.

Earth from Israel
At this time people believed that a god could only be worshipped on their "home" land. In order to carry on worshipping God, Naaman asks Elisha if he can take some of the earth of the Promised Land home with him to make a holy place in Syria.

> ❖ **ABOUT THE STORY** ❖
> *It was important that Elisha and Gehazi did not take any gifts, because Naaman needed to learn that God does not do things for people just because they are generous. God's love, forgiveness and help cannot be bought. The healing is an example of what the Bible calls grace – God's undeserved and unearned kindness. This story reminds us that God loves everyone, including those we consider to be enemies.*

Saved from the Syrians

THE king of Israel relied on Elisha to help him with the continuing Syrian attacks. The prophet sent detailed warnings to the palace, outlining the Syrians' battle plans. He'd tell the king exactly where and when the Syrians would hit next, so the Israelites were always ready.

The Syrian king grew frustrated. "It's as if the king of Israel can read my mind!" he raged.

"Elisha the prophet knows the secrets you whisper in your bedchamber," his servants replied. "It's he who tells the king."

"He has to be stopped!" the king roared. "Where is he?"

"In the Israelite city of Dothan," came the answer.

"Go there at once and seize him," the king bellowed.

In Dothan, Elisha's servant woke up and flung open the door. "Master, master, look!" he screamed. "The Syrian army is right here, in Dothan!"

Stretching into the distance were gleaming chariots and armoured men. "Never mind," he reassured Gehazi. "There are more of us than there are of them." Elisha prayed, and Gehazi could see chariots and horses of fire all around their house. Then Elisha prayed again. "Lord, please strike the Syrians blind – just temporarily." And he set off down to the Syrian camp.

Samaria
This piece of ivory furniture from Samaria is decorated with a carving of a lion fighting with a bull. The city was besieged and captured by the Assyrians in 722BC and this signalled the end of the northern kingdom of Israel.

Siege craft
During a siege, the attacking army surrounded the city. The army would try to cut off supplies of food and force the inhabitants to surrender.

The blinded Syrians were stumbling about, terrified. When Elisha arrived and told them to follow him, they were only too pleased to hear someone who seemed to know what was going on, and they marched on until Elisha told them to stop. There was a short silence while he prayed, and then suddenly the soldiers found they could see again. To their horror they found they were in Samaria, the capital city of Israel.

The King of Israel was just as confused as the troops. "What shall I do?" he asked Elisha. "Shall I kill them?"

> ## 66 The king said to Elisha, 'My father, shall I slay them?' 99

"No," laughed the prophet. "Show how great you are by giving them a huge feast and then sending them all home."

After that the Syrians didn't attack Israel again for a long time. But eventually King Benhadad decided to lay siege to Samaria and starve the Israelites into defeat so he surrounded the city. No one could get in or out. Traders and merchants bringing food and wine to the city were turned away, and people got hungrier and hungrier.

Inside Samaria, things grew desperate. The people would eat anything – weeds, mice, beetles. Each day the Israelite king walked around the city walls. When he even saw people arguing over eating each other, he stormed off to Elisha. "Your God has done this to us!" he yelled.

"Tomorrow there will be plenty of food on sale in this city, and all at the right price," Elisha yelled back. "Trust me." Then he began to pray.

Later that night, four starving lepers sneaked out of the city to the Syrian camp. They were dying anyway, so weren't risking much by asking the enemy for food. But they couldn't see a soul or hear a sound. The camp was deserted.

The Lord had filled the ears of every soldier in the camp with the sound of a mighty army on the move. Thinking that a huge army of Israelite reinforcements was heading straight for them, the panicking soldiers hadn't hung about to strike camp. They had just fled, leaving everything exactly where it was.

The lepers went wild, dashing from one storehouse to the next, shoving food into their mouths, cramming it into their pockets, running off and hiding it. Then they thought they'd better go and tell the king. And the next day, food was on sale in Samaria just as Elisha had said – more than enough for everyone.

The journeys of Elisha
After Elisha witnessed Elijah being carried to heaven by the flaming chariot, he travelled around a great deal, but he spent a lot of time in Samaria. In the capital city of Israel he brought God's message to the kings and people. It was near Samaria that Elisha's servant saw the vision of the heavenly army.

❖ ABOUT THE STORY ❖
In the days of Elisha there were far fewer maps. Most people who travelled had little idea what the places they were aiming for looked like. The roads were mostly tracks and there were no signposts. So the Syrians were blind in the sense that they were lost! Also, they didn't really know what Elisha looked like – there were no photographs – so they didn't recognize him. They hardly expected their enemy to walk up and introduce himself!

Jehu the Avenger

A commander in the Israelite army called Jehu was sitting in the officers' room one day when a messenger came from Elisha, asking to talk to him in private. Jehu took the rather agitated man out of the room. The man took out a bottle of sacred oil and said, "I anoint you king of Israel. You will strike down every last one of the royal family belonging to King Ahab, fulfilling the great Elijah's prophecy." Then he dashed away.

Now Jehu knew that King Joram of Israel, Ahab's son, lay very ill in bed, but he certainly wasn't dead yet. And why ever would he, Jehu, be chosen as the next king?

"Is everything all right?" his friends asked, as he returned pale-faced to the mess.

"Yes, everything's fine," Jehu replied, his mind obviously elsewhere.

"So why did that mad fellow come to see you then?" the other officers began. They pressed him so hard to find out what had happened, that eventually Jehu gave in and told them. Roaring with delight, they laid their cloaks down so Jehu wouldn't have to get his feet dirty, and took him out to show the other soldiers. They trumpeted loud fanfares to proclaim Jehu their new ruler, then raced off to get rid of King Joram.

The king's guard on the watchtower in Jezreel looked down and saw a group of charioteers in the distance, speeding towards the city in a cloud of dust. The racing chariots showed no sign of slowing, and the lookout soldiers guessed that Jehu was at their head – he was well

known for driving everywhere at top speed.

King Joram realized that if one of his highest-ranking officers was dashing to see him, it must be serious; and he raised himself up out of his sick bed to go out and meet him.

"You're too ill to go alone," said Joram's nephew, King Ahaziah of Judah, who had come to visit his sick uncle. "I insist on coming too."

Joram was too weak to argue. "Prepare our royal chariots," he croaked to his servants, as he staggered out on Ahaziah's arm.

Face to face the chariots thundered nearer and nearer. When they were within shouting distance, King Joram gathered his remaining strength and yelled, "Do you come in peace, Jehu?"

"How can I come in peace," came the reply, "when your mother, Queen Jezebel, is worshipping idols, practising black magic and leading our whole country into sin?"

Joram's heart began to pound. "Treachery, Ahaziah!" he cried, and the two kings wheeled their chariots back in the direction of the palace. But it was too late. Jehu reined his horses to a halt, drew his bow and fired an arrow that pierced Joram right between the shoulder blades. The king sank down dead in his chariot and his driverless horses careered over the bumpy ground. Jehu paused just long enough to order his men to catch the chariot and fling Joram's body on to the ground, abandoning it to the birds and the

beasts. Then he pursued the fleeing king of Judah and shot him dead, too.

Next, Jehu turned back to the city of Jezreel. Queen Jezebel was waiting for him at the palace, adorned in her finest regalia and hanging over the balcony, screaming insults. Jehu looked up at the trembling servants who stood next to her. "Are you with me?" he shouted. The men didn't hesitate to please their new king. They grabbed hold of the queen and hurled her out of the window.

Jehu had had a busy day. He strode into the palace and instructed the servants to prepare him something to eat and drink. He rested and ate his meal, recovering from his exertions. By the time he felt refreshed enough to get round to ordering the servants to clear away the queen's body, stray dogs had eaten her and there was nothing left.

> ❝ *Jehu slew all that remained of the house of Ahab in Jezreel.* ❞

The avenging king's work wasn't over. During the months that followed, he ordered his officers to bring him the heads of all of Ahab's 70 other sons. Then he laid plans to kill all Ahab's counsellors, friends and priests. Finally, the whole of King Ahab's house lay dead, just as Elijah had prophesied.

Face at the window
This ivory carving is believed by some to be Jezebel looking out of her palace at Jezreel.

EHU WAS FOLLOWING GOD'S ORDERS WHEN HE WENT OUT AND TOOK REVENGE ON AHAB'S FAMILY FOR ALL THE WRONG THEY HAD DONE. IT IS NATURAL FOR PEOPLE TO FEEL ANGRY ABOUT THOSE WHO DO WRONG. THE NEW TESTAMENT SAYS THAT FOLLOWERS OF JESUS ARE NOT TO TAKE REVENGE LIKE THIS. THERE'S A BETTER BUT MUCH HARDER WAY TO RID THE WORLD OF EVIL: BY LOVING OUR ENEMIES.

❖ ABOUT THE STORY ❖

This bloodthirsty story comes from a time in history when there was not the kind of legal and police system we have today. People who were wronged had to take revenge themselves. Ahab and Jezebel broke God's law so blatantly that God took His revenge through Jehu, and there was no way he could be stopped. This story shows that Ahab and his supporters got what they deserved in the end.

The End of Israel

KING Benhadad of Syria was ill – so ill that he thought he might be dying. He remembered how the Israelite prophet Elisha had cured Naaman of leprosy, and told his servant, Hazael, to ask him if it was God's will that he should recover, too.

Elisha knew just why Hazael had come. "You can tell your king that he will get better," the prophet said, "but God has told me that he's going to die." Hazael was more than a little confused by this answer, but he didn't question it because Elisha was staring at him so strangely. Then the prophet began to weep. "I am grieving because you will bring great suffering to Israel," Elisha explained. "You will set on fire our fortresses, slay our men, batter our women to death and crush our children."

Hazael was appalled. "What am I, a wild animal?".

"You are to be the next king of Syria," Elisha said quietly.

On the long journey back to Damascus, Hazael had plenty of time to think about what the prophet had said. The day after he returned, he took a blanket and suffocated Benhadad while he slept. Then he took the throne for himself.

Meanwhile, in Israel, King Jehu was busy putting right the wrongs of King Ahab and his son King Joram. He did his best to wipe out the worship of Baal and other pagan gods from his land, directing his subjects back to the Lord. But he didn't go quite far enough. He allowed King Jeroboam's two golden calves to remain on their altars at Bethel and Dan. And the Lord began to punish Israel, using the king of Syria to do so. Hazael continually attacked Israel and took more and more land. When Jehu and Hazael died, their sons carried on in their footsteps. Jehu's son Jehoahaz continued the worship of the calves at Bethel and Dan, and angered the Lord still further. In turn, God continued to give Hazael's son military success. The king of Syria slaughtered so many of Jehoahaz's

❧ ABOUT THE STORY ❧

The fall of Israel was a very sad event. The ten northern tribes were never re-united. The Bible writers say that this last defeat was God's punishment for the nation's refusal to worship Him alone, and for people's desire to follow wrong religious practices. The end was a long time coming, however; God had warned them for several centuries. This story shows that God is a judge, but that He is also very patient.

Bowing to the king
This limestone relief shows Jehu, or one of the ambassadors of the king, bowing down in front of the conquering King Shalmaneser, which was the usual gesture of defeat. Behind the kneeling figure, Israelite attendants carry the gifts requested by Shalmaneser. The stone dates from around 840BC and originally stood at Nimrud in Assyria.

Winged sphinx
This statue of a winged sphinx was a common image in Assyrian art. Statues like this were put at the gates of their palaces as they believed they had the power to ward off evil spirits.

troops that in the end there were no more than 10,000 foot soldiers, 50 horsemen and 10 chariots left in the Israelite army. By the time King Jehoahaz died, the whole land of Israel was very nearly destroyed by the might of the Syrian army.

It was left to Jehoahaz's son, King Jehoash, to fight back. By now Elisha was a very old man. As he lay dying, he called Jehoash to him for the last time. "Take a bow and arrows and open the window to the east," the frail prophet asked Jehoash. Then Elisha laid his hands over the king's hands and told him to shoot an arrow out of the window in the direction of Syria. "That is the Lord's arrow of victory, the victory you shall have over your enemy," the holy man told him. "Now take the other arrows and strike the floor with them." Jehoash hit them on the floor three times. Elisha's face fell. "You should have struck more times, for then you would have defeated Syria completely," he told the king. "Now you will win only three battles." Nevertheless, these three battles were enough to recover several Israelite cities and keep the Syrians at bay.

Over the years that followed, the Israelites fell back into worshipping pagan gods and ignoring the Lord. Weird idols and strange altars reappeared all over the countryside, with all sorts of seances, black magic and even human sacrifice taking place. And the Lord made

sure that each Israelite king had an increasingly hard struggle to hold on to his lands.

> ❝ *So Israel was exiled from their own land to Assyria.* ❞

At the same time, a greater threat than Syria was rising: the cruel, merciless Assyrian Empire. They conquered country after country, and soon the Assyrian King Shalmaneser turned his eyes towards the Promised Land. Shalmaneser said he would leave Israel alone as long as King Hoshea, the last king of Israel, paid the Assyrians a vast amount of gold and silver each year. The desperate Hoshea sent messengers to Egypt begging for help, but Shalmaneser heard of his plot and the vast Assyrian army swooped down to lay siege to Samaria. The capital city was besieged for three nightmarish years before it finally fell. The kingdom of Israel was no more.

The Assyrians rounded up the Israelites and scattered them across their empire. Samaria became filled with foreigners from other lands conquered by the Assyrians. They became known as Samaritans.

Idol worship
The Samarian golden calves were set up by Jeroboam, the first king of the divided Israel, to try to stop his subjects going to the temple in Jerusalem to worship.

Assyrian Empire
The Assyrian Empire, at its height, stretched across the whole of the 'fertile crescent'. This is a crescent-shaped area of land that is very good for growing all kinds of crops. The crescent followed the routes of the three great rivers of the area: the river Nile in Egypt, and the rivers Tigris and Euphrates in present-day Iraq.

Kings of Judah

WHEN Jehu the avenger killed King Ahaziah it left the kingdom of Judah without a ruler. The king's mother, Athaliah, wanted to be queen. So she set about killing everyone else in the royal family. Soon, Athaliah ruled unchallenged over Judah – or so she thought. For an heir still remained. Ahaziah's sister had smuggled one of his sons, Joash, into the temple in Jerusalem, where her husband, Jehoiada, was high priest. There the little boy grew up unharmed, while his grandmother wreaked havoc as queen.

When Prince Joash was seven years old, Jehoiada

told his secret to the senior army officers and some elders of Judah. Under heavy guard, the young boy was crowned the new king of Judah.

"Treason!" Athaliah cried, when she saw her subjects bowing to the child. Jehoiada told the guards to take her out of the temple, and they killed her in her own home.

At first Joash was a good king who loved the Lord. He was upset that the temple built by Solomon had fallen into disrepair, so he set up a collection box for donations of money to restore the building. But when the high priest died, evil officials talked Joash into worshipping pagan idols. The king even sent money from the temple fund to King Hazael of Syria, to pay him not to attack. Prophets warned the king that his sins would bring Judah down, but he refused to listen. Once, Jehoiada's son, Zechariah, climbed to the top of the temple and began preaching. "Why have you all forsaken the Lord?" Zechariah shouted. "God says that because you've abandoned Him, He's going to abandon you."

Leprosy
This picture shows King Uzziah in the temple, burning incense on an incense altar. For this sin, he was struck down with leprosy. Today, leprosy is known as a contagious disease that affects the skin, the inside of the mouth and the nerves. The Hebrew word for leprosy is less specific. Some of the features of leprosy described in the Bible do not occur in the disease that we call leprosy today.

Household gods
This is a statue of an Assyrian god called Lahmu, which means 'the hairy one'. Lahmu was one of the household gods who guarded homes and kept out evil spirits. The Assyrians put figures of these gods under the floors of their houses. Lahmu is just one example of the pagan gods the Judeans turned to at this time.

The crowds began to drag Zechariah down. King Joash chose not to call a stop to the riot. Instead, he watched as the prophet was beaten to death. The king went to check he was really dead. Zechariah's eyes suddenly opened. "May the Lord see and avenge!" he whispered.

That year the Syrians attacked Jerusalem. They slaughtered many people and plundered the capital. Joash was killed by his own men. They knew that he had brought the trouble upon them.

Under Joash's son, King Amaziah, the country went from bad to worse. He worshipped pagan idols as well as the Lord. And instead of attacking Syria, he turned on his neighbour, Israel. As God's punishment, Judah was defeated and Amaziah captured. The wall of Jerusalem was broken and the treasures in the temple seized.

Amaziah's son, King Uzziah, determined to do better. He worshipped only God, and the Lord helped his army win many victories over his enemies. But success went to his head and Uzziah grew arrogant. When he tried to burn incense in the temple, a job only priests were allowed to do, the Lord punished him by striking him with leprosy.

> ❝ *And the Lord smote the king, so that he was a leper to the day of his death.* ❞

Uzziah's grandson, Ahaz, was the worst king of all. He abandoned all pretence of worshipping the Lord and turned openly to worshipping the pagan gods. He worshipped idols and even burned his own son alive as a sacrifice. He smashed all the holy objects in the great temple in Jerusalem and replaced the great altar with a pagan one, then he eventually locked its doors forever.

God was furious. First He allowed the king of Syria to march into Judah and take hundreds of captives back with him into Damascus. Then He let the king of Israel massacre Judah's army and return to Samaria with over 200,000 prisoners. Other tribes in the Promised Land such as the Edomites and the Philistines took towns and villages in Judah. Eventually Ahaz found himself facing the might of the ruthless Assyrian King Tiglath-Pileser.

❧ ABOUT THE STORY ❧

The kings of Judah had a great advantage over the kings of Israel – the temple was in their capital to remind them of God and His laws. But even good kings were weak, led astray by their officials and forgetting that God had helped them succeed. These stories are in the Bible to show how important it is for leaders to live in God's ways. When they don't, the whole country suffers.

King Tiglath-Pileser
This stone relief from Nimrud in Assyria shows King Tiglath-Pileser standing in his chariot with a driver and an attendant. The relief dates from around 740BC.

Damascus
The kingdoms of Israel and Judah were often attacked by the Syrians, and many of their treasures ended up in Damascus, the Syrian capital. This picture shows goods for sale in modern-day Damascus.

Isaiah Shows the Way

IN the year that King Uzziah died, the prophet Isaiah had a vision in the temple. He saw the Lord sitting on a throne. Above Him were angels called seraphim who sang a beautiful song in praise of God:

"Holy, holy, holy is the Lord of hosts, The whole earth is full of His glory." The temple trembled and was filled with clouds of smoke.

> 66 *'Holy, holy, holy is the Lord of hosts.'* 99

"Help!" cried Isaiah. "I have seen the King, the Lord of hosts. How can I live with being the sinning, flawed person I was before?"

One of the seraphim flew to the prophet, touching his lips with a burning coal that he'd taken from the altar. "Your sins have been forgiven," the angel told him.

Then came a voice that made Isaiah's heart leap. "Who is there that will take my message for me?" God asked.

Without a moment's hesitation, the eager prophet sprang to his feet. "Here I am, Lord!" he cried. "Send me."

"Then go and speak to my people," said the Lord. "But you will find they will not listen or understand till they have been scattered far from the Promised Land."

God spoke to the prophet throughout his lifetime. He spoke of trouble, but also of great hope. "For to us a child is born," Isaiah said, joyfully, "to us a son is given." He was speaking of the coming Messiah, Saviour of the world.

ISAIAH'S VISION REVEALED GOD'S HOLINESS – HIS PERFECTION. BIBLE WRITERS TELL US THAT GOD CAN NEVER DO WRONG, AND THAT WE ARE TO TRY TO BECOME LIKE GOD, HOLY IN SPEECH AND CONDUCT. ∽

Seraph
A seraph has six wings, two to fly, and a pair each to cover its face and feet. The task of the seraphim Isaiah saw was to guard the throne of God.

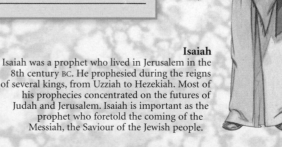

Isaiah
Isaiah was a prophet who lived in Jerusalem in the 8th century BC. He prophesied during the reigns of several kings, from Uzziah to Hezekiah. Most of his prophecies concentrated on the futures of Judah and Jerusalem. Isaiah is important as the prophet who foretold the coming of the Messiah, the Saviour of the Jewish people.

King Hezekiah the Good

JUDAH had held out against the Assyrians for 20 years after Israel had been conquered. God was rewarding Judah's good king, Hezekiah, who had destroyed all the pagan altars and kept the Lord's laws. Then the Assyrian king, Sennacherib finally attacked. Hezekiah was afraid and offered Sennacherib all his gold and silver to keep out of Jerusalem. Hezekiah even had to strip the temple itself in order to make the payment. But the ruthless Assyrian went back on his word and marched on Jerusalem anyway.

Sennacherib's spokesman tried to talk the citizens into surrendering, speaking in Hebrew, to make sure that everyone understood. "Hezekiah may say that your God will save you, but no nation has been saved from the Assyrians by their god. Make peace instead," he shouted.

The king told his subjects not to listen to the Assyrian lies, and went to the temple to pray. "Don't worry," Isaiah told him. "The Assyrians will never be allowed to enter Jerusalem, for it is God's city and he will certainly defend it."

That night, the Lord sent an angel over the Assyrian camp, and many of Sennacherib's troops died. Then news came that the African country of Ethiopia had suddenly attacked Assyria and the king was needed back home. And on returning to his capital, Nineveh, Sennacherib was murdered by his sons.

The saving of Jerusalem was not the only miracle God worked for the good Hezekiah. Once, when the king was very ill and was near death, he begged the Lord to repay his faithfulness with a little more life. Isaiah brought the news that his prayers had been answered, God was granting him 15 more years of life.

But no matter how hard the king tried not to sin, he could not lead a blameless life. Years later, when the king of Babylon's son came to visit, Hezekiah proudly boasted about all the treasures he once again possessed. He showed the pagan prince every single precious gem, piece of gold and chest of spice he owned.

Isaiah was not pleased. "God says the time will come when all you have shown to this prince will be carried off to his kingdom," he prophesied, "and your sons will be servants in the Babylonian king's palace."

God's angel of death
This medieval-style picture shows an angel flying over the Assyrian camp, striking the soldiers dead. God sent the angel to save the king of Judah, Hezekiah, because he had been a faithful worshipper of God.

❧ **ABOUT THE STORY** ❧

This story shows that God is completely fair and just in every possible way. When Hezekiah most needs the care and support of the Lord, God is there for him, and is able to give him as much extra life as He wishes, to reward Hezekiah for his loyalty. But when Hezekiah makes a mistake, he is punished by God. It may seem harsh to punish the king for this mistake, but God has very high standards of behaviour for all His people.

Josiah and the Law

WHEN King Hezekiah of Judah died, his 12-year-old son, Manasseh, came to the throne. Manasseh was as bad as his father had been good. He not only rebuilt all the pagan altars that Hezekiah had destroyed, but built new ones too. He even set up statues of idols in Jerusalem's great temple! He had witches and wizards as counsellors and he took part in all sorts of evil rituals.

The next king, Amon, was just as wicked and cruel as his father. The people killed him, and put his eight-year-old son Josiah on the throne instead.

Like his great-grandfather, Hezekiah, Josiah loved God even when he was a very young boy. It saddened him to see how the temple had been dishonoured and vandalised over the years, and at the age of 26 he ordered the great house of the Lord to be repaired.

Craftsmen cleared every dusty corner, restoring the building wherever possible, and knocking down and rebuilding wherever it was not. Sacred objects, that had been flung aside for years, again saw the light of day and were polished up, good as new.

One day, the high priest, Hilkiah found a soft cloth. Inside a hole was a bundle wrapped in richly embroidered material. When Hilkiah unwrapped the package, he gasped. Inside lay an ancient scroll containing laws that God had given to Moses long ago in the wilderness. Trembling, he took it straight to the king.

Josiah read the scroll at once. He didn't stop until he'd taken in every single word. And he was horrified. King after king in Judah had led the people in breaking every law there was to break. And the scroll told of the dreadful punishments that God promised to those who sinned. Josiah broke down and wept, tearing his hair and ripping his clothes. "My people!" he cried. "Is it too late to be forgiven for our sins?" The king sent his officials to ask a prophetess, Huldah, what he could do to put things right. Her answer was solemn: "All you have read in the holy scroll will come true. Your people have sinned and the Lord will take vengeance upon them. But because you are full of repentance, God will allow you to live in peace. Your eyes will not see the misery of Judah's punishment."

> **And when the king heard the words of the book of the law, he rent his clothes.**

Josiah ordered everyone in Judah to come to a great meeting at the temple. Loud and clear, Josiah read the scroll of the law to his subjects. His face was stern, his eyes deadly serious. You could have heard a pin drop. Not a sneeze, not a cough, not a whisper came from the huge throng while the king was reading. Then Josiah rolled up

Scroll of law
The Hebrew laws, also called the law of Moses, are God's instructions to His people as to how they must worship God and live their lives.

Josiah and Huldah
This picture shows Josiah's officials asking advice from the prophetess, Huldah, as to how they could make amends for past errors.

At last, the Lord was the one and only God worshipped in Josiah's kingdom, and the king led his people in a festival which had been forgotten for many years – the feast of the Passover – which they celebrated just as it said in the scroll of the law. Everyone in the country spoke about the wonderful things the young king had done. But it was not to last, because 13 years later Josiah was killed in battle and his reforms were to die with him.

the scroll and held it aloft, so everyone could see. "From this day onward," he thundered, "I swear with all my heart and soul to live by every single law in this scroll and walk in the path of the one true God." The crowds before him leapt to their feet. "We are with you!" they cried. "We will obey the Lord!"

Then Josiah told the priests to burn the pagan idols in public. He ordered all the heathen priests in Judah to be slain, and then went the length and breadth of the country, smashing every single one of their altars into dust. He cleared the places where human sacrifices had been offered and filled them with the bones of the dead, and no one went there any more.

Josiah
This picture shows Josiah reading the scroll. Although Judah was ruled by Assyria, their hold on the land was weakening. This meant Josiah could ignore the Assyrian gods he was told to worship.

Assyrian bronze demon
This is a bronze statue of an Assyrian demon, called Pazuzu, who was believed to carry disease. It is 15cm high and dates from around 800BC.

✜ ABOUT THE STORY ✜

In this story Josiah tries to make up for the way that his father and grandfather led the people away from God. When Hilkiah finds the scroll of the Laws of Moses, Josiah is determined to reform the people of Judah. While he is alive he inspires his people to live as God wants them to, but Huldah the prophetess makes it clear that Judah has to be punished, and the reforms are lost when Josiah dies.

Jeremiah's Warnings

JEREMIAH was the son of a priest, and a quiet young man. He was stunned when he heard the Lord talking to him. "I want you to speak for me to the people," God said, "to remind them what dreadful fates will befall them if they continue to do wrong. It will be difficult, because they won't want to listen and they won't believe you. But don't get downhearted. Tell them everything I say, and I will give you the strength to cope."

The Lord told Jeremiah to go to a potter's house and watch him moulding his clay. As the wheel span, the water jar the potter was making suddenly collapsed into an ugly, squat shape. The potter stopped what he was doing and squashed the clay into a wet ball. Then he threw it back on to the wheel and began again, shaping it into another quite different vessel that stood tall and upright and beautiful. "Go and tell the people of Judah that they are like clay in my hands," the Lord told Jeremiah. "At any time, I can crush a nation that is becoming evil and destroy it. But if it repents, I can change my mind and allow it to flourish into something strong and good."

Jeremiah bought one of the potter's earthen flasks and set out for the valley of Hinnom, where many of the locals had turned once again to pagan worship. In front of all the people, he raised the flask up above his head and then dashed it to the ground, where it smashed loudly into a thousand tiny pieces. "The Lord says that the day is coming when this place will be called the Valley of Slaughter," he cried. "Because you have forsaken the one true God, your enemies will slay you here in your homes. The Lord will shatter Judah like this broken flask, so no one can repair the kingdom."

So Jeremiah's mission began, travelling from village to village with the same message, for the Lord wanted to give His people one last chance to mend their ways. But everywhere he went, he was shouted down by the angry locals and chased out of town – some of them even tried to kill him. Yet the lonely prophet didn't give up, and the Lord gave him enough courage to stand and preach in Jerusalem in the temple itself: "Listen to the word of God!" he shouted, above all the jeers and insults. "The Lord will destroy this very city and all the towns through the whole of Judah. For you stubborn, stupid people are refusing to heed his warnings."

> **'Behold, like the clay in the potter's hand, so are you in my hand, O house of Israel.'**

The high priest, Pashhur, pushed his way through the mob. "How dare you cause this commotion in the house of the Lord!" he spat, striking and kicking Jeremiah until he lay cowering on the ground, and then hauling him away for a night in the stocks. But Jeremiah had a personal prophecy ready for Pashhur when he came to release him the following morning: "The Lord says that you will bring terror onto yourself and onto all your friends. Your enemies will kill all those you love while you look on, helpless. Judah will fall into the hands of the king of Babylon, and you, Pashhur, and all your family shall be carried away to live there in captivity. You will die in exile for failing to lead the people in the true ways of the Lord."

When God saw that Jeremiah wasn't having much success with talking to the people, He told him to write down every single word He'd said on a scroll. Perhaps then the warnings would seem more 'official' and the people might take notice of them. So Jeremiah called his loyal servant, Baruch, and dictated everything God had ever said to him. It was a long and tricky job. Everything had to be remembered perfectly and written down just so. But finally it was finished. "Baruch, you must read this to the

people," Jeremiah told the exhausted scribe. "I can't do it; I am not allowed to go to the temple. If I do the officials will arrest me. Go to the temple and, slowly and clearly, read out the whole scroll. Don't miss out anything."

One of the men who heard Baruch reading in the temple was Micaiah, a high-ranking official in the king's government. The words left him shaking in his shoes and he went straight to the royal court to tell his superiors what he'd heard. Baruch was immediately sent for and told to read the scroll all over again. The nobles were just as worried as Micaiah. "Are you sure this has all come from the mouth of the man of God?" they asked.

"Every word came from Jeremiah's lips and was written down by my hand," Baruch assured them.

"Then go and hide with your master, out of reach of King Jehoiakim's anger," the nobles urged him. They took the scroll to the king's secretary for safekeeping, and nervously went to Jehoiakim's chamber to tell him the most importants bits. To their surprise, the king seemed to take it all quite calmly. "Really?" he remarked, looking concerned. "All Jeremiah's work, eh? He says it's the word of God, does he?"

When the king asked if he could see the scroll for himself, the nobles were pleased. "Of course," they agreed. "We're so glad you're taking an interest in it. We really do feel that there's something in these words of Jeremiah's." But to the nobles' horror, as each chapter of the scroll was read out to the king, Jehoiakim merely cut it off and threw it into the fire.

And when the last piece had burned away, the king sighed and wiped his hands. "That's sorted that," he said.

The Lord spoke to Jeremiah. "Never mind," He consoled the dejected prophet. "You'll just have to write it all out on a new scroll." And Jeremiah began to dictate to Baruch all over again.

Jeremiah

Jeremiah is seen here with his scribe, Baruch. Jeremiah was first called as a prophet in his early twenties. His prophesying continued for 40 years and spanned the reigns of the last five kings of Judah: Josiah, Jehoahaz, Jehoiakim, Jeconiah and Zedekiah. Jeremiah's prophecies did not always please the kings and priests of the time and, as a result, he was persecuted, plotted against and imprisoned. He spent much of his life struggling with the dilemmas that his prophetic calling imposed upon him.

❖ ABOUT THE STORY ❖

Jeremiah is sometimes called 'the weeping prophet'. The state of his country and the attitudes of the people upset him terribly. His message was not all doom and gloom; he offered hope to people who trusted God. The fact that he was made to suffer by people who rejected his message reminds later readers that following and serving God is sometimes very hard. It is sometimes necessary to face imprisonment and even death.

The End of Judah

KING Nebuchadnezzar of Babylon conquered nation after nation, growing so strong that he crushed even the mighty Assyrian Empire. He swept into Judah and surrounded Jerusalem, leaving King Jeconiah (Jehoiakim's brother) begging for mercy. Nebuchadnezzar agreed to leave Judah alone, but on drastic terms. First, Jeconiah and the royal family would be taken into captivity in Babylon, along with all the elders and priests. Secondly, Nebuchadnezzar would also take into exile many of Judah's skilled craftspeople, whom he could use in his own kingdom. Thirdly, Judah would have to pay a massive yearly tribute of treasure in return for peace. And fourthly, Nebuchadnezzar got to choose his own king: the youngest of the good King Josiah's sons, Zedekiah, who would have to obey his every word if Judah was to be left alone.

The stunned people left in Judah could hardly believe what had happened. They were deeply shocked at losing their leaders, and their own future hung in the balance.

Jeremiah wrote a letter of comfort to the exiled people in Babylon: "God says make the most of this bad situation. Do all your usual things and enjoy life. Don't grumble and be nasty to the Babylonians. Look after their cities and the Lord will look after you. For He has told me that in 70 years' time, He will bring you back to the Promised Land where you will again live happily."

Jeremiah started wearing an oxen's harness to show the people in Judah that being captured by the Babylonians was not a bad thing. They would be happy living under someone else's rule, as the ox was. "This is the Lord's work," the prophet said. "Judah's punishment is unfolding as it should."

The Lord showed the prophet a vision of two baskets outside the temple: one full of plump, juicy figs and the other full of overripe, stinking fruit. "The exiles in Babylon will eventually ask me for forgiveness and I will make sure that they flourish like the good figs," God explained. "But anyone who struggles against my will and tries to remain in Judah will rot like the fruit in the second basket." After this, Jeremiah went to King Zedekiah himself to warn him to put all thoughts of rebellion out of his head. "You must not try to resist Nebuchadnezzar," he warned, "or you will lose everything."

"Just whose side do you think you're on?" cried Zedekiah, and locked him up. But Jeremiah's faith didn't waver. He believed that the Lord would one day restore Judah and, to prove it, he invested a large sum of money in buying a piece of land.

I have given all these lands into the hand of Nebuchadnezzar, the king of Babylon

Even under house arrest, Jeremiah kept on sending out messages. "Anyone who stays in Jerusalem will die by sword, starvation and disease," he told them. "But those taken into exile by the Babylonians will live and prosper."

"This is ridiculous," thought the nobles of Jerusalem, "we have to shut him up." They threw Jeremiah into a deep, dark, mud-filled pit and left him there to die. But the king secretly sent a servant to haul him out and bring Jeremiah to him. "I need you to tell me the truth," he said to the prophet in private.

"Promise not to kill me and I will," replied the exhausted, starving prophet. The king anxiously agreed.

"God says that if you surrender to Nebuchadnezzar, the lives of you and your family will be spared and this city will survive," said Jeremiah. "However, if you try to fight against the Babylonians, Jerusalem will be burned to the ground and you will not escape from their hand."

Several years later, despite all Jeremiah's warnings, Zedekiah made a deal with the Egyptian army to try to defeat King Nebuchadnezzar and the Babylonian army. But the Egyptian king went back on his word and withdrew his troops, leaving Jerusalem to stand alone. The Babylonians pounced and Zedekiah barricaded the city. It withstood the siege for two years before the starving people finally gave in. The king was caught and forced to watch his sons slaughtered before he was blinded. He was led in chains to Babylon, along with many of his subjects. Only a few of the very poorest people were allowed to remain in Judah. Nebuchadnezzar's army smashed the walls and pulled down the temple before burning the city, just as Jeremiah had said they would.

Babylonian Empire
After the Assyrian Empire, the Babylonians became the greatest military force in the region. They conquered the Assyrians to occupy the important area of fertile ground around the River Tigris in the east, and the River Jordan in the west.

❧ ABOUT THE STORY ❧

The final destruction of Jerusalem took place in 587BC. This incident is one of the most important in the whole of the Old Testament. It marks the end of Judah as an independent country; there were never again any real kings to rule it and it was always dominated by a larger nation. Its destruction showed people that God had meant what He said – He hated rebellion against Him.

Ezekiel and the Exiles

WHEN the Babylonians were taking their captives from Judah into exile, they asked Jeremiah whether he would like to go or stay. Times were dangerous in the tiny, weak country, and he chose to stay to help Gedaliah, the governor the Babylonians had appointed to rule over the few people who remained. But the pagan tribe of the Ammonites saw their chance to take back land they had lost centuries ago to Moses and Joshua and they murdered Gedaliah. "Stand your ground against the Ammonites," Jeremiah told the terrified Judeans. "If you remain in Judah, the Lord will one day make you strong again. But if you are tempted by the thought of fleeing to Egypt, and wilfully abandon the Promised Land, you'll have only

death to look forward to." But the people of Judah fled, forcing Jeremiah to go with them, and the last remnants of the nation were swallowed up by the Egyptian civilization.

Meanwhile, among the exiled people of Judah – now called "Jews" by the Babylonians – a new prophet had arisen, a man called Ezekiel. Before Jerusalem had fallen, the Lord had told him that it would be up to him to try to keep the Jews together as a nation and turn them back to the one true God.

It was an extremely difficult task. The Jews were now scattered throughout a foreign country, among a strange people who had their own religions and customs. The Jews had no Promised Land, no elders, no kings. And the great temple in Jerusalem, where they thought God lived, had been destroyed.

Ezekiel had to teach the Jews two very important lessons – first, that God is everywhere, and secondly, that God judges everyone on who, not what, they are. For at first the Jews thought that simply being one of God's race of chosen people was enough to be given back the Promised Land one day.

"Here you are among pagans," Ezekiel said. "You're worshipping their idols, eating their food and sacrificing to their gods. Do you really think that the Lord will reward you? Each one of you is responsible for yourselves. If your father has sinned, you won't necessarily be damned for it. If your children commit crimes, God won't consider it to be your fault. The Lord is here, watching you in exile, and judging each one of you on your own, purely on what you do and how you live."

Ezekiel
The prophet Ezekiel was taken to Babylon as an exile. Five years after this, he received his call as a prophet. His prophecies were not generally popular but he still managed to reach a position of honour.

The Exile
This map shows Babylon, where the exiles were taken. This was a very important time in the history of the Israelites. In Babylon, under the leadership of prophets like Ezekiel, they became a united nation. This was where they were first called Jews.

> *As I prophesied, there was a noise, and behold, a rattling; and the bones came together, bone to its bone.*

Gradually, the Jews began to take Ezekiel's teaching to heart. Far from their homeland, living among strangers and surrounded by foreign religions, they began to pull together as a nation and turn back to worshipping the one true God. And as soon as they did so, they began to enjoy life and prosper, just as Jeremiah had hoped they would. Jewish craftsmen began to be recognized for their skilled work. Jewish farmers were employed by Babylonian landowners at excellent rates of pay, and Jewish officials rose to prominent positions in government.

God was pleased and he began to grant Ezekiel visions of the restoration of the Jewish people and the rebuilding of the temple in the Promised Land. "The Lord has shown me that our nation lies dead like a skeleton," Ezekiel told the people. "But we have only to ask God to breathe on us and we will live. The scattered parts of the skeleton will connect together, bone to bone. And the Lord will join the two peoples of the Promised Land into one kingdom with one king, and raise us up to life as one nation."

❧ ABOUT THE STORY ❧

Prophets like Jeremiah had been told by God that the Israelites would prosper living in Babylon, and also that the nation of the Jews would be properly created after the Israelites had been taken far from their homeland. Under the leadership of Ezekiel this begins to happen. God's long term plan for his chosen people is coming to fruition, and the Jews are learning to love God and live by his laws, and they are reaping the benefits.

The father of Judaism
This picture shows Ezekiel teaching the Jews in exile. He is thought of as the founding father of Judaism as it is today, as it was he who drew together the exiles from Israel and Judah and made them into a faithful and devoted people.

Nebuchadnezzar's Dream

IT wasn't just God who was pleased with the way the Jews worked hard and lived good lives in Babylon. King Nebuchadnezzar was pleased too. So pleased that he took the most promising young people to the palace to learn Babylonian culture and language.

Four of the students were Daniel, Shadrach, Meshach and Abednego. They worked hard and God rewarded them with exceptional talents in letters and wisdom, and the gift of understanding dreams for Daniel. At the end of the course they amazed the king who gave them important jobs on his royal staff.

The king often had bad dreams and would ask his advisers to tell him what they meant. These "wise men" consulted oracles and conjured up spirits, then told Nebuchadnezzar what they thought he wanted to hear. But after one dream the king decided to test them. "This time, I don't just want an interpretation," he said. "I want you to tell me what I dreamed, too."

Panicking, the advisers made a wild stab at lying. The king was enraged. "Put them all to death!" he fumed. Unfortunately, that included Daniel and his three friends. When Daniel heard, he ran to the king. "I'm sure I can tell you about your dream," he begged.

Nebuchadnezzar remembered how Daniel had impressed him before. "Come back tomorrow," he demanded, and Daniel dashed home to pray.

Next day, he returned confidently. "No human, however wise, can tell you your dream," Daniel began. "But last night the Lord showed me. You dreamed of a huge statue –

Brick-making
The furnace in the story was probably used for making bricks. A brick is a piece of straw and mud or clay (usually rectangular) that is dried hard in the sun or baked in a kiln. In Bible times, bricks were used more than any other material for building. At first, bricks were shaped by hand, but later wooden moulds were used. In Babylon, bricks were often stamped with the king's name. The picture, from a tomb near Thebes, shows brick-makers at work.

Book of Daniel
This is a fragment on a Greek papyrus manuscript of the book of Daniel from around AD250. This Greek version of the Hebrew Old Testament originally contained the books of Ezekiel, Daniel and Esther and was one of 11 books from a Christian library found in Egypt.

the head was gold, the chest and arms silver, the belly bronze, the legs iron and the feet half iron, half clay. A huge rock smashed the statue into pieces that blew away on the wind. Then the rock grew into a great mountain which filled the world." Nebuchadnezzar gasped. "The body parts stand for five empires," Daniel explained, "that will come after yours. But God's kingdom will eventually destroy all human empires and will stand for ever."

> " *The mystery was revealed to Daniel in a vision of the night...* "

After that, Daniel was appointed chief royal adviser and his three friends were made provincial governors. The other district officials were filled with jealousy. But they didn't have long to wait to get their own back.

Nebuchadnezzar made a huge golden statue. He ordered a fanfare to be played at certain times, and whenever the people heard the music, they were to fall down in the direction of the idol and worship it – or be thrown in a furnace. The jealous district officials told Nebuchadnezzar that Shadrach, Meshach and Abednego refused to pay homage. They were arrested and brought to Nineveh.

"Do what you will. We cannot bow down to an idol," the friends told the king. The king ordered that the furnace be made seven times hotter than usual, and that the friends should be bound and thrown into the blazing furnace immediately.

But when Nebuchadnezzar went to check that the men had been burned to a cinder, he was utterly baffled. The servants who had thrown the Jews into the white hot flames were killed by the searing heat. But inside the furnace, the three men were walking around freely, chatting to what looked like an angel. "Come out!" Nebuchadnezzar roared. The three men stepped out of the blaze without a single hair on their head singed.

The shocked king sent a decree through the whole of Babylon. "No one may say anything against the God of the Jews, for no other god is as powerful as theirs."

The meaning of the dream
The kingdoms described in Daniel's interpretation are believed to be Babylon (represented by gold), Persia (silver), Greece (bronze) and Rome (iron). The rock that grew into a huge mountain represents the everlasting kingdom of God.

❖ ABOUT THE STORY ❖

These stories were included in the Bible to encourage the exiles to stand firm for God and not to lose their faith when they were being threatened in Babylon. The stories showed that God could save His people from terrible things, just as He had done in the past. People in ancient times were very interested in dreams; Daniel's experience reminded them that God understood everything even if people did not.

Belshazzar's Feast

THE next king to seize the Babylonian throne was Belshazzar. He loved to show off just as much as Nebuchadnezzar, and was especially fond of holding massive feasts to impress everyone. Belshazzar planned one grand banquet for a thousand guests. The huge banqueting hall was decorated with the richest hangings and ornaments from the royal treasure houses. Hundreds of waiters, musicians and dancers were booked. Belshazzar employed the very best chefs in Babylon and brought rare delicacies from the furthest corners of his empire for their elaborate menus. He ordered the most expensive wines from his cellars. The king took care of every single detail.

The feast was a complete success. The guests applauded and cheered the performance of the entertainers. They gasped as the waiters brought in platters of magnificent food and placed jewelled pitchers of wine on every table. Then Belshazzar called for silence. "Ladies and gentlemen," he announced proudly, "tonight is a very special night. You are in the greatest city in the world, being entertained by Nineveh's top performers, tasting the best food and wine that money can buy." Belshazzar's guests gave a loud cheer. "It is only right," the king continued, "that you should be eating and drinking from the finest plates and cups." Belshazzar turned to his servants. "Bring out the holy goblets we mighty Babylonians took from the Jews' temple in Jerusalem!"

The guests loved it. "Let's drink to our own gods!" they cried, drunkenly. "Here's to the gods of gold and silver!" They turned to toast the king himself and raised their glasses. "Cheers Belsha..." Their voices died away as they saw that the king was pale-faced and still, staring like a statue at a mysterious hand writing on the wall. The ghostly finger traced several words and Belshazzar sank wobbly-legged into his seat. "Guards! Guards!" he cried. "Fetch my advisers immediately!"

Belshazzar's magicians were totally baffled. Not one of them could tell what the mysterious writing said. "Call Daniel," advised the queen mother. "My husband Nebuchadnezzar used to say he was the wisest man in the entire world."

> " *They drank wine, and praised the gods of gold and silver.* "

The king promised to make Daniel the third most important man in the empire. "Keep your promotion," replied Daniel. "You're not going to be pleased with what I have to tell you. The first word – *mene* or 'number' – means that you have reached the full number of days God is granting you as king. The second word – *tekel* or 'weight' – means that God has weighed out what you are worth in His eyes, and it isn't much. The third word – *parsin* or 'divided' – means that your kingdom will eventually be split up. God is going to give half to the Medes and half to the Persians."

The party was definitely over. That very night, King Belshazzar was murdered. And Cyrus, king of the Medes, took the empire of Babylon for himself.

MANY PEOPLE TAKE FAITH IN GOD LIGHTLY AND MAKE FUN OF PEOPLE WHO WORSHIP GOD. THIS STORY REMINDS BELIEVERS THAT ONE DAY GOD WILL JUDGE EVERYONE ON EARTH. ∽

Hanging Gardens
The Hanging Gardens of Babylon did not literally 'hang', but were built on the roof on stepped levels called terraces. King Nebuchadnezzar is said to have built the gardens to please his wife, who missed the greenery of her home in the mountains of Media. The Hanging Gardens were well known throughout the ancient world and in the 2nd century BC were listed as one of the Seven Wonders of the World.

Persian Empire
The Persian Empire stretched from Egypt in the west right across to the banks of the river Indus in what is modern Pakistan. Persia was the largest of the three empires, the others being Assyria and Babylonia, that ruled Palestine and beyond.

Return from Exile

KING Cyrus was a man with new ideas of how to run an empire. He told all the peoples who had been captured by the Babylonians that they were free to go home. He had a special message for the Jews. "It is your God who has made me emperor over all the earth. Now go and rebuild His house in Jerusalem. Anyone who wishes to remain in Babylon can help by giving money and supplies to those who are returning." Cyrus even gave back the treasures Nebuchadnezzar had taken from the temple.

Not all the Jews wanted to leave. They had been in exile for many years, and a lot of them knew no other life than in Babylon. But some began to pack. The prophets Isaiah, Jeremiah and Ezekiel had foretold that the Jews would one day rebuild Jerusalem, and they decided that now the time had come, it was up to them to do it.

The Jews found Jerusalem still in ruins. They built an altar out in the open air for the Feast of Tabernacles, and offered prayers and sacrifices. Then work on the temple began under two new leaders: Jeshua (a priest) and Zerubbabel (a descendant of King David). The day the foundations were finished was a day of great emotion. The priests led the celebrations with singing and dancing, and there were tears of sadness from those who remembered the former great temple of Solomon, as well as tears of joy.

> " *The returned exiles celebrated the dedication of this house of God with joy.* "

The work went on, very slowly. The peoples brought to the Promised Land by the conquering Assyrians and Babylonians came to look. "We want to help," they volunteered. "We've been following your religion as best we can. Let us help with the building and then we can all worship your God together." But the Jews wouldn't have any of it. During their years in exile, they'd followed their religion very strictly. They were afraid that if they let foreigners join in – some of whom still worshipped pagan idols – they would be led into breaking

Samaritans
After the Assyrians captured Samaria and the Israelites were sent away, Samaria was filled with people from other lands who became known as Samaritans. The Jews always resented them for taking their kingdom. Here the Jews are sending away the Samaritans.

❖ **ABOUT THE STORY** ❖

The exiles returned from Babylon to Jerusalem in 538BC, but the temple was not finished until 516BC – almost exactly 70 years after Nebuchadnezzar had destroyed it. This was the second Jewish temple to stand in Jersualem; the Temple of Solomon was the first. The second temple was not as big or grand as Solomon's first temple. It stood until the Roman General Pompey destroyed it in 63BC.

some of their laws. "You can have nothing to do with our God or our temple," the Jews told the Samaritans. The rioting that broke out was so bad that the exiles were forced to down tools, and the temple was left unfinished.

With the passing years, times grew harder in the Promised Land. "Look at what's happening," a prophet called Haggai told the Jews. "Our crops are failing, the water is drying up, our clothes are falling to bits and money seems to run through our fingers. It's because we've built ourselves houses to live in, but we haven't finished off the house of the Lord."

"The Lord has told me that we should be strong and complete the building of the temple," another prophet, Zechariah, agreed. "He says that as soon as we've done it, there'll be bumper harvests and plenty of rain, and we'll live peacefully and prosper."

This encouraged the Jews to go back to work. But the envious Samaritans went to the governor of the province to cause trouble. "Who gave you permission to build here?" he demanded angrily.

"We're building at the command of Emperor Cyrus himself," the Jewish elders explained. "If you write to the new king, Darius, he'll tell you it's the truth." When the governor received a reply from Nineveh that, yes, Darius had indeed found such a decree signed by Cyrus, the Samaritans were forced to back off and the temple was finally finished. The Jews celebrated by holding the great feast of Passover and sacrificed 12 goats among the many offerings – one for each of the scattered tribes of the Promised Land. At last, the surviving Jews felt they had made a new beginning.

Palestine after exile
When the Jews returned to Israel their great ideas for rebuilding the city and the temple gradually became less important. They felt that building houses and farming the land for food were more urgent. The prophet Haggai reminded them that God would care for them if they rebuilt the temple in His honour.

Haggai's message
The prophet Haggai told the Jews that their lives would not improve until they got their priorities right and started putting God first, instead of themselves.

Rebuilding Jerusalem

THE Promised Land remained a province of the empire of the Medes and Persians for many years, under Darius's successor King Ahasuerus and then King Artaxerxes. Stories about the few Jews who had left the comfort and security of Babylon and had returned to their homeland used to make their way across the empire to the many people who had stayed in Babylon and Persia. The news was not always good. Rumours reached a priest called Ezra that the Jews in Israel were slipping into bad habits, mixing with the pagans and becoming lazy in their worship of the Lord. He at once begged the Persian King Artaxerxes to let him go to sort it out. Now Ezra was very persuasive. The king found himself not only giving permission for Ezra, his fellow priests and a couple of thousand Jews to return to the Promised Land, but also found himself giving money to help them on their way. He wrote an official decree that told the provincial governor to support Ezra in any laws and judgments he thought fit to impose on the people.

The minute Ezra arrived in the Promised Land, people came running to him to tell of Jews who had married into the pagan communities and were living according to their ungodly customs – it turned out that the priests and the community leaders were the worst offenders of all! Ezra sat down in front of the temple and wept, crying out in a loud voice, confessing everything the people had done wrong. It was as bad as he had feared. But the determined holy man didn't stay downhearted. He made the priests swear to amend their ways and called everyone to attend a meeting of the utmost importance. Soon a crowd of Jews stood in the open square of the temple, while Ezra told them in no uncertain terms that they had to give up everything to do with pagans and turn back to God's law.

It wasn't just Ezra whom King Artaxerxes allowed to return to the Promised Land with his blessing. Some years later the king noticed that his butler was moping around with a long face and he asked him what was wrong.

"Sir, I've heard that my countrymen, the Jews, have raised a new temple in Jerusalem," Nehemiah explained. "But the city all around it is a disgrace. It's still lying utterly in ruins."

> **Come, let us build the wall of Jerusalem, that we may no longer suffer in disgrace.**

"I shall write a letter to the provincial governor, Sanballat, to tell him that I'm putting you in charge of rebuilding the city, and you must go at once," said the king. "Just promise me that you'll come back as soon as you've finished."

Of course, Sanballat and Tobiah, his second-in-command, gave Nehemiah a very frosty reception. The king had sent them a Jew who had been given equal powers to their own, and they had been given no part to play in the rebuilding of the important walled city. Nehemiah knew from the start that the government officials were going to make life difficult for him, so he surveyed the ruins of Jerusalem late at night, sorting out in secret what needed to be done.

As soon as Nehemiah got down to work, Sanballat and Tobiah did their best to cause trouble. First, in front of the provincial army, they taunted and ridiculed the Jews as they scuttled back and forth over the charred heaps of rubble. Then, as the walls began to take shape, they tried different tactics. "The ramparts and turrets are for shutting you out of the city," the officials told the local people, trying to make them angry. "Are you going to just sit back and watch?"

Sanballat and Tobiah were delighted when the furious Samaritans began to attack the workers on the walls at every opportunity. But Nehemiah simply split the working Jews up into teams, and put two teams on each shift: one to stand watch with weapons and fight if necessary, the other team to carry on building the walls.

Under Nehemiah's leadership, the Israelites finished the walls in only 52 days. Even the local people who had tried to tear them down were impressed. "Their God must have had a hand in it," they whispered, as they stood beneath the towering walls in awe and watched the Jews sing and dance their way right round the city in a great ceremony of dedication.

While the Jews were completing the inside of the city, they didn't take any risks with the Samaritans, who were getting more and more worried as the city neared completion. Each day, they kept the gates firmly shut against attack as they built house after house, until there were enough people living inside Jerusalem to defend it. Then, just as Sanballat and Tobiah had feared, they cast out anyone who wasn't Jewish through and through. At last the descendants of the kingdoms of Israel and Judah felt they could hold their heads up high again. They were back in the Promised Land, one nation under one God.

Ahasuerus and Darius
This section of a stone relief shows the Persian King Darius on his throne. Behind him stands his son, Ahasuerus, who was also known as Xerxes. This relief was found in Persepolis, in Iran. It is around 2.5m high and dates from 521 to 486BC.

❖ ABOUT THE STORY ❖
Nehemiah is one of the great heroes of faith in the Bible. His job in Persia was very important – he had to make sure the king wasn't given poisoned wine! He combined his practical common sense with a deep faith in God which he expressed through prayer. Whenever a problem arose, Nehemiah didn't just think up a solution, he prayed for God's help and wisdom too.

Daniel and the Lions

DANIEL was one of the Jews who felt too old and settled to leave Babylon. Instead of returning to the Promised Land, Daniel remained at the palace, a trusted adviser to King Cyrus of the Medes and Persians. Cyrus's successor, King Darius, relied on Daniel even more. Darius made Daniel one of the most powerful people in the whole empire. He appointed him as one of three ministers to rule over his kingdom. Daniel did a much better job than the others. Darius began to trust him more, consulting him privately and giving him special responsibilities. The two other ministers were jealous. They began to seek a way to bring about Daniel's downfall, eager to find any little mistake they could blow up into something big. But Daniel was such a God-fearing man that he seemed to live a perfect life. He didn't lie or swear. He didn't gossip and spread rumours. He always dealt with people fairly, and was polite and helpful. The two ministers were soon at their wits' end.

They plotted together, and went to King Darius with a clever plan. "We need a new law," one of the men told him, looking serious. "Nobody should be allowed to ask for anything from any god or man except you for a period of 30 days."

"And anyone who breaks the law should be flung into a den of lions," added the second, eagerly. "All the district officials agree."

"Oh all right then," Darius sighed, stamping his royal seal on the law. The two men hurried away to spy on Daniel, rubbing their hands with glee.

It wasn't long before they were back at the palace, demanding to see the king.

"We think you should know about Daniel," they said. "He gets down on his knees three times a day and prays to his God, facing Jerusalem. What are you going to do about it?"

King Darius realized he had been tricked and was furious. "Get out of my sight!" he roared, kicking

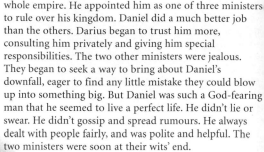

King Cyrus
This marble head from the 6th century BC shows King Cyrus, who ruled Persia from 558 to 530BC. It was Cyrus who conquered the Medes in 549BC.

Medes and Persians
This stone relief dating from around 485 to 465BC shows a row of Medes and Persians. The Medes are wearing rounded hats and short tunics, whereas the Persians are dressed in full-length robes and tall crowns.

the two ministers as they grovelled before him. The worried king spent all day striding back and forth, desperately trying to think of a way to get Daniel off the hook. But it was no good.

"The law's the law," the officials insisted.

So Darius very reluctantly sent his guards to arrest his best minister.

The king shuddered as he stood at the top of the pit, listening to the lions roaring hungrily below. He turned to the old man who stood beside him and placed his hand on his arm. "Daniel, my friend," he said to his trusted adviser. "May your God – whom you serve so faithfully – save you." The royal guards lowered Daniel down towards the snarling lions, then blocked off the pit with a huge stone. Darius marked the entrance with his royal seal, so no one would dare tamper with it, and then trudged back to the palace. The sad and anxious king wouldn't eat or talk to anyone. He shut himself up in his room and spent a sleepless night alone, worrying, and furious that he'd been tricked by his ministers.

> 66 *The king said to Daniel, 'May your God, whom you serve continually, deliver you.'* 99

As soon as the sun rose, Darius was back at the pit, demanding it be uncovered. "Are you down there, Daniel?" he cried, as the guards began heaving away the stone. "Are you all right?"

To his great relief, a familiar voice came floating up from the darkness. "My king, I am alive. An angel has been here with me, and the lions have done me no harm."

The emperor nearly wept with joy. "Quick," he yelled at his guards. "Get him out of there at once!"

Later on, the lions got their dinner after all. The king ordered that the two wicked ministers be thrown into the pit along with their families, and the animals tore them to bits. Then Darius sent a proclamation out to every corner of the Medean empire announcing to all the nations that Daniel's God should be worshipped by everyone as the one true God. "He saves all of those who believe in Him," wrote the emperor, "and His kingdom will last for ever."

Lion of Babylon
This picture shows a detail from a reconstruction of the gateway into Babylon. Lions were associated with kings and power.

Marduk
In this picture from a carved cylinder found at Babylon, the Babylonian god, Marduk, is shown standing on a creature which has the body of a serpent. This creature was his symbol. Marduk wears a crown and holds a rod and a ring, which are symbols of authority.

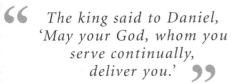

❧ ABOUT THE STORY ❧

The book of Daniel was written especially to encourage Jews to be faithful to God at a time when they were being persecuted by people who did not believe in God. No one finds it easy to admit they believe in God when they know they could be killed for it. Daniel's example was meant to show them that even in such terrible situations, God could still help and rescue them, but that even if He didn't, they should still be faithful to Him.

Esther the Beautiful

DURING the reign of the next emperor, King Xerxes, there were still many thousands more Jews living in Babylon and Persia than had returned to the Promised Land. The civilization of the Medes and Persians was still the greatest in the world, and Xerxes was immensely proud of his empire, which stretched all the way from India to Ethiopia. He decided to hold a massive banquet in his capital, Susa, to celebrate his magnificence. First, he invited every single one of the princes, army chiefs, nobles and governors in his empire to a feast the likes of which no one had ever seen before. In immense marble halls bedecked with banners of the finest silks, his honoured guests lay on golden couches and ate off jewelled platters while every single one of the priceless valuables in Xerxes' treasure houses were paraded before them on velvet cushions. It took 180 days for the stunned VIPs to admire all Xerxes' splendours. Then the generous king threw his doors open to his subjects too, holding a magnificent garden party for a further week in the grounds of the palace itself. The ordinary people were stunned, they had never seen such magnificence! There were refreshing fountains tinkling in the sunshine, the perfume of sweet-smelling flowerbeds, mosaics underfoot of mother-of-pearl and precious stones – and as much free wine as everyone could drink!

By the seventh day the king was feeling exceedingly merry. "I've not only got the most beautiful palace in the world," he thought, "I've also got the most beautiful queen too." He summoned his seven chamberlains and ordered them to go and fetch the queen at once. "Tell her to put on her best dress," he demanded. "I want to show her off to everyone."

Now Queen Vashti was giving her own party for all the women, in another part of the palace. She was a strong, independent woman, besides being beautiful, and she refused to come. "I can't leave my guests so rudely," she told the chamberlains. "Whatever would they think? And besides, I don't want to be paraded about like something from one of my husband's treasure houses."

When the chamberlains told the king that Vashti wouldn't come, he was mad. Xerxes' courtiers were far too frightened of the raging emperor to tell him to calm down. In fact, they all nodded their heads and agreed that he was very right to be so angry. "Whatever are you going to do about Vashti?" the most senior of them urged. "You can't possibly let her go unpunished. What will happen if other women get to hear of it? We'll have wives all through the empire rebelling against their husbands. And where will that leave us?"

> " *Let the maiden who pleases the king be queen instead of Vashti.* "

"You're right," decided Xerxes. "Vashti will have to go. Kick her out and find me a new queen to take her place – one who's even more beautiful."

A royal proclamation soon went out through all the land, announcing a competition. All the young maidens in

the kingdom were to present themselves at the palace. The most beautiful would be chosen to stay for lessons in skincare, hairstyling, make-up and how to behave like a queen. And at the end of a year, the king would choose the one he liked best to replace Vashti.

In the back streets of Susa there lived a servant in the royal household called Mordecai, an old Jewish man who was one of those who had chosen to stay in Babylon rather than return to the Promised Land. Mordecai was the guardian of his orphaned cousin Esther, whom he had brought up as his daughter. "No one could be more beautiful or queenly than you," he told her, giving her a hug. "Hurry along to the king's palace and enter the competition– but make sure you don't tell anyone you're Jewish. The king might not be so keen on that."

Esther easily made it on to the short list of the most beautiful maidens in the country and she was hurried off to new living quarters in the palace, where all the young women were to be groomed for a year. Every day, Mordecai would make sure he had an errand to do that would take him past her chambers. And every day, he was more and more pleased with what he saw of Esther's progress. She was such a well-mannered and good-natured girl that she quickly became the favourite of Hegai, the courtier in charge of the competition. He made sure that Esther had the very best face creams, the finest food from the royal kitchens and the most skilled maids to help her with her hair and advise her on her clothes.

The time came for the young women to parade, one by one, in front of the king. They were all trying very hard to impress him. In the end, though, there wasn't much of a competition at all. Esther was by far the winner, and the delighted Xerxes held a lavish great banquet in honour of his lovely new queen.

Make-up and jewellery
Wealthy women wore jewellery, like this gold armlet which is decorated with griffins, a mythical animal with an eagle's head and a lion's body.

THIS STORY SOUNDS A BIT LIKE THE STORY OF CINDERELLA – SOMEONE FINDING THEIR DREAMS COME TRUE, AND GETTING FAMOUS AND RICH. BUT THIS STORY IS NOT JUST ABOUT ESTHER HAVING FUN AND ENJOYING HER NEW ROYAL LIFE. IT REMINDS US THAT WHEN GOD DOES ALLOW SUCH THINGS, HE GIVES US RESPONSIBILITIES TOO. ESTHER WOULD HAVE A VERY DIFFICULT, BUT ALSO IMPORTANT, JOB TO DO AS QUEEN.

⚜ ABOUT THE STORY ⚜

This story is really about God's protection of His people and the timing of His purposes. It seemed pure chance that Esther was chosen, and she kept very quiet about her nationality. But God knew that soon she would be the only person who could avert a tragedy. The Bible shows God working behind the scenes so that everyone is in the right place at the right time when it really matters.

Esther Saves the Jews

NOT long after Esther had become queen, Mordecai heard two palace servants in the palace plotting to kill the king. He hurried to tell his daughter and she went straight to her husband. Xerxes ordered the men to be arrested, tried and hanged.

After this, the king decided he could do with a right-hand man. He chose Haman, who was an arrogant man who ordered everyone to bow when they saw him coming.

"I'm not paying homage to anyone but God," Mordecai said. Haman wanted revenge for being embarrased. He decided to punish not only Mordecai, but his entire race.

"Sir," Haman said to Xerxes one day, "there's a people in your empire who refuse to live by your laws. They ignore your government officials and only take notice of their own priests and elders.

If you don't put a stop to it, you'll soon have a full-scale rebellion on your hands. Why don't you let me exterminate them?"

"Order what you think best," Xerxes said, handing him his royal seal. "Have these troublemakers wiped out."

"The prime minister's proclamation includes you," Mordecai wrote to Esther. "Go to your husband and beg him to do something."

But it wasn't that simple. Esther replied, "It's the death penalty for anyone who enters the king's presence uninvited. But if I am to die for my people, then so be it."

After three days of fasting and praying, the brave young queen went to the king. Luckily his face brightened into a smile. "What can I do for you?" he said, and held out his sceptre to her, ushering her in.

Festival of Purim
The Jewish festival of Purim is held in spring to commemorate the defeat of Haman's plot to massacre the Jews. At the festival, the book of Esther is read aloud and it is customary for the congregation in the synagogue to cheer Esther's name, but shout and boo whenever Haman is mentioned.

The king's sceptre
Esther was risking her life when she went to see the king. This was an offence punishable by death, unless the king held out his sceptre. This law allowed the king some privacy and protected him from would-be murderers.

Casting lots
Haman threw lots, rather like modern dice, to determine a day to carry out his plan to exterminate the Jews. Small stones and pieces of pottery, like the ones above, were often used as lots. The word *purim* is the plural of the word *pur*, which means "lot".

"Sir," Esther said, "will you have dinner with me tomorrow? And will you bring the prime minister?"

The king was delighted. Haman smirked smugly.

"No one else in the entire empire is as important!" he bragged to his friends. But one thought left him glowering. "Still that Mordecai refuses to bow."

"Don't put up with it," everyone urged. "Get the king to build a gallows and hang him. Then you can enjoy tomorrow's dinner unspoilt."

The king had been unable to sleep and he'd been reading his official records all night. "Look here," Xerxes remarked to his advisers, "there's no record of how we rewarded Mordecai for foiling that murder plot. We must put things right straightaway." The King called Haman. "If you were king, how would you reward your most loyal servant?" the king asked.

> " *And Haman said to himself, 'Whom would the king delight to honour more than me?'* "

Haman thought the king was talking about him. "Dress the hero in your robes and crown and set him on your horse. Then give him a parade through the streets with a noble leading the way, shouting, 'The king is delighted to honour this man!'" he said.

The king clapped his hands. "Brilliant!" he cried. "Hurry along and do it for Mordecai the Jew."

It was the beginning of the end for the miserable Haman. That night, at dinner, Esther made her plea. "Oh my king, I am Jewish," she sobbed, "and orders have been given for me and my people to be put to death."

Xerxes was outraged. "Whose orders?" he bellowed.

"His!" Esther wept, pointing at the evil prime minister. Just as Haman had wanted, the king demanded that gallows to be built as quickly as possible – but it was the prime minister who was hanged on them, not Mordecai. Esther confessed that the faithful servant was her foster father and Xerxes rewarded him with Haman's old job. At once, Mordecai sent out an edict which cancelled the former prime minister's commands and, thanks to Esther, thousands of Jewish lives were saved.

ESTHER PUT GOD AND OTHERS BEFORE HERSELF. SHE COULD HAVE DONE NOTHING AND DIED WITH HER PEOPLE. INSTEAD, SHE RISKED HERSELF TO SAVE THEM. IT IS AN EXAMPLE OF HOW GOD WANTS US TO LIVE.

Esther
This painting shows Queen Esther dressed in her royal robes. She was very brave and risked her life to save her people. But the Bible does not commend her when she encourages the Jews to massacre their enemies.

❖ ABOUT THE STORY ❖
The Medes and Persians had very strict laws. Once a law was made, no one – not even the king – could change it. So when Haman was hanged, the order to kill the Jews still stood. The new law which Mordecai drafted allowed the Jews to defend themselves against anyone who attacked them. That way, no one would bother to comply with the original law.

Jonah and the Whale

IN the days of the great Assyrian Empire, there was a prophet, Jonah, who was not very pleased when God called him. "Jonah, I want you to go to the Assyrian capital, Nineveh," the Lord told him. "Preach to the pagans there. They're doing nothing but sinning against me." Now Nineveh was a long way away, the Assyrians were a hard, cruel race and Jonah – a Jew – didn't really care about foreigners anyway. "I'll run away to somewhere the Lord can't find me," he thought, packing a bag. Soon he was boarding a ship and setting off on a long voyage in quite the opposite direction to Nineveh – to Tarshish in Spain.

No sooner had the ship left harbour and reached open waters than the skies darkened and the wind began to blow up. Great gusts whipped up the sea, rain lashed the masts and the ship was tossed up and down the towering waves, threatening to break up at any moment. Terrified, the sailors threw as much of their cargo overboard as they could to lighten the load, but the ship still bowed and cracked in the full force of the storm. "On your knees!" cried the captain. "Each one of you beg your gods to save us!" and he ran around the ship to check that everyone was praying.

Then the sailors superstitiously cast lots to find out which of the passengers had brought the wrath of the gods upon them. They picked Jonah, who was soon surrounded by the angry crew. "Which god do you serve?" they demanded. "What have you done to bring this storm raging down upon us?"

"I'm a Hebrew," Jonah gulped. "The only thing that's going to save everyone is if you throw me overboard." Even though the sailors were desperate, they weren't murderers, and they did their best to row to shore. But it was impossible. With every stroke of their oars, the wind seemed to blow more strongly. In the end, they had no choice but reluctantly to throw Jonah off the ship. As soon as the prophet had splashed into the water, the gale began to die down and the waves to subside. And as Jonah drifted away from the ship on the swell, he heard the captain and the sailors praying once more – but this time to the one true Lord, not to their pagan gods.

> " ... and Jonah was in the belly of the fish three days and three nights. "

Just when Jonah thought things couldn't get any worse, they did. One minute he was bobbing up and down in the water like a cork; the next minute, he was swimming around inside a dark, wet cave – a huge fish had swallowed him up. For three days and nights Jonah was in the pitch black darkness of its belly. "Oh Lord," he prayed, "I'm dreadfully sorry. If you get me out of here, I promise to obey you in future." A little circle of light appeared in the distance and very quickly widened. There was a rumbling and a roaring and a rushing of water, and the fish coughed him out of its mouth. Choking and spluttering, the prophet felt himself dropped onto a firm bed of sand. "Thanks be to God!" he cried as the waters drew back leaving him in warm sunlight blinking on the dry land.

happened. The sun set on the 40th day and still nothing had happened. "We have been saved," cried the people of Nineveh. "God has forgiven us!" They sang and danced and rejoiced, offering prayers and sacrifices to God – all except Jonah, who stomped off into the desert.

"Why have you spared them, Lord?" he moaned up to heaven, stacking a few sticks together as a shelter from the heat. "They aren't even Jewish! If you're going to save sinners like these, I'd rather be dead than serve you."

God taught Jonah one last lesson. Overnight, a broad, shady tree grew over Jonah that guarded him from the burning sun till evening and kept him cool. But next morning, the disappointed prophet found that the tree had withered away. And Jonah needed its protection more than ever. All day long, not only did the sun blaze down but a scorching wind also blew across the sands. "Lord, the death of that tree is the last straw," Jonah groaned. "Please let me die."

"How can you be so upset about the death of a tree you didn't plant or water," the Lord scolded, "when you're cross with me for not killing the thousands of people in Nineveh?" Jonah finally realized that God created all the people of the world, and He cares for people from all nations, not just his own; that the Lord's kingdom stretches over the whole earth.

The Lord's voice boomed at him: "Now are you ready to go to Nineveh for me? Tell those pagans that unless they beg my forgiveness for their sins, in 40 days' time I will destroy the city." Jonah trembled before the power of God, and set off at once.

The city of Nineveh was so big that it took Jonah three whole days to work his way across it, shouting himself hoarse as he went. But to his great surprise, the ruthless Assyrians listened to what he had to say. When the king himself got to hear Jonah's message, he sent out a royal proclamation ordering everyone to begin praying and fasting at once. When dawn broke on the 40th day nothing

A reluctant prophet
Jonah tried to escape from the purpose that God had for him by fleeing on a boat from the port of Joppa. He could not escape the will of God, though, and when the sailors threw him overboard to try to save their ship, he was swallowed by a big fish, which left him on the shore. From there he went to Nineveh.

❧ ABOUT THE STORY ❧

The point of this story is that God cares about people of all races and wants everyone to love and worship Him. Jonah started with a very narrow view of God's purposes. He thought that God had given the Jews, and the Jews alone, the right to be saved. Jonah's experience changed his view. This story also encourages people to obey God even when they don't see the reasons for the instructions. Everything will always work out as God intends.

The Old Testament Prophets

ELIJAH was a prophet of Israel who lived in the 9th century BC, during the reign of King Ahab. Nothing really is known about his background. Six episodes in the life of Elijah are related in the Bible: his prediction of drought, the contest on Mount Carmel, his flight to Mount Horeb, also called Mount Sinai, the story of Naboth, the oracle about King Ahaziah, and Elijah's ascent to heaven. All these episodes, except for the last, are concerned with the clash between the worship of the God of Israel and that of Baal. It was King Ahab's wife, Jezebel, a Phoenician princess, who encouraged Baal worship among the Israelites.

In the first episode, after Elijah announces to King Ahab that there will be a drought, he escapes, first to the brook at Cherith and then to Zarephath, in Phoenicia, where he performs a miracle by healing a sick boy. In both places God provides for Elijah.

In the second episode, Elijah presides over a contest between God and Baal on Mount Carmel. Elijah's sacrifice to God bursts into flames, whereas the sacrifice of Baal's priests remains unlit. After this victory, there is a mighty storm as God puts an end to the drought by bringing the rain. In doing so, He shows Himself to be superior to Baal.

Elijah then flees to Mount Horeb, the mountain where God gave Moses the Ten Commandments. Elijah's journey to this holy place is important as Elijah is returning to one of the most important places in the Jewish faith.

The fourth episode tells the story of a man called Naboth. He refuses to sell his vineyard to King Ahab because he knows it is forbidden by God to sell inherited land. When Ahab has Naboth stoned to death and takes his vineyard, Elijah announces that he will be punished.

In the fifth episode, Elijah reveals that God will punish King Ahaziah for worshipping the Syrian god, Baal-zebub.

Finally, Elijah is taken up to heaven in a chariot of fire and his role as prophet passes to Elisha.

It was Elijah that was to appear to Jesus, along with Moses in what is called the Transfiguration. Elijah remains to this day one of the most important of the Old Testament prophets; a place is still set for him at the table for some of the Jewish feasts.

Elijah and Moses
Elijah has been compared with Moses. Elijah is accompanied and succeeded by Elisha, just as Moses was by Joshua. Elijah's demonstration of God's power on Carmel was like Moses receiving the law on Mount Horeb.

The chariot of fire
This picture shows Elijah being taken away to heaven in a chariot, watched by Elisha. The taking of someone to heaven, while still alive, is called a translation. Only two people in the Bible are said not to die: Elijah and Enoch.

ISAIAH was a prophet in Judah from around 740-700 BC. Most of his prophecies concentrated on Judah and, in particular, on its capital, Jerusalem. He prophesied from the reign of King Uzziah to the reign of King Hezekiah.

These were troubled times for the Jewish people as, not long after Isaiah was called as a prophet, the Assyrians took over the state of Judah, making it part of their empire.

Isaiah's prophetic life began when he had a vision in the temple at Jerusalem, of God sitting on a throne, surrounded by angels called seraphim. God told him to go out and speak to the people, passing on the message that they should put their trust in Him alone, they should not worship other gods, they should keep His laws, and should listen to His prophets.

Isaiah's vision
Isaiah had a holy vision of Jesus in a kingdom where the wolf would lie down with the lamb.

From ancient times, Isaiah has been thought of as the greatest of all the Old Testament prophets. He has been called, amongst other things, "the prophet of holiness" and "the eagle among the prophets". He is perhaps most important as the prophet who foretold the birth of the Messiah, who would be descended from King David and would come to save the Jewish people. Isaiah prophesied that the present Assyrian Empire of violent rule would be replaced by a peaceful kingdom of God. He described the Messiah as a king of Israel who would free his people from the Assyrians. Christians, though, believe that Isaiah's words foretell the coming of Jesus Christ, who would save everyone, Jews and Gentiles alike, from sin.

Isaiah says, "For unto us a child is born, unto us a son is given: and the government shall be upon His shoulder: and His name shall be called Wonderful, Counsellor, the mighty God, the everlasting Father, the Prince of Peace."

❧ KINGS OF ISRAEL AND JUDAH ❧

The single nation ruled by Saul, David and Solomon split into two after Solomon died.

Israel (north)	Judah (south)
Jeroboam 931-910BC	Rehoboam 931-913BC
Nadab 910-909BC	Abijah 913-911BC
Baasha 909-886BC	Asa 911-870BC
Elah 886-885BC	Jehoshaphat 870-848BC
Omri 885-874BC	Jehoram 848-841BC
Ahab 874-853BC	Ahaziah 841BC
Ahaziah 853-852BC	Athaliah 841-835BC
Joram 852-841BC	Joash 835-796BC
Jehu 841-814BC	Amaziah 796-767BC
Jehoahaz 814-798BC	Uzziah 791-740BC
Jehoash 798-782BC	Jotham 750-732BC
Jeroboam II 793-753BC	Ahaz 735-716BC
Zechariah 753-752BC	Hezekiah 729-687BC
Shallum 752-752BC	Manasseh 696-643BC
Menahem 752-742BC	Amon 643-640BC
Pekahiah 742-740BC	Josiah 640-609BC
Pekah 752-732BC	Jehoahaz 609-609BC
Hoshea 732-723BC	Jehoiakim 609-597BC
	Jehoiachin 597-597BC
All dates for kings	Jeconiah 597-597BC
are approximate.	Zedekiah 597-587BC

❧ PROPHETS ❧

The Old Testament prophets worked in specific regions. Some even prophesied in foreign countries.

Israel	Judah
Samuel 1050-1010BC	Joel 810-750BC
Elijah 870-852BC	Isaiah 740-700BC
Micaiah 870-852BC	Micah 742-687BC
Elisha 855-798BC	Zephaniah 640-610BC
Amos 760–780BC	Huldah 610-605BC
Hosea 760-722BC	Habakkuk 605BC
	Jeremiah 626-587BC
All dates for prophets	Ezekiel 593-570BC
are approximate.	Nahum 630-612BC

Jeremiah   Ezekiel   Samuel   Micaiah

The Book of Psalms

THE Book of Psalms in the Old Testament, also known as the Psalter, is a collection of 150 religious verses which are sung or recited in both Christian and Jewish worship. According to tradition, 73 of the psalms were written by King David, a musician and a poet. Other authors named in the titles are King Solomon and the prophet Moses.

*O Lord, our Lord, how majestic is Thy name in
all the earth!*

*Thou whose glory above the heavens is chanted
By the mouth of babes and infants, Thou hast founded a
bulwark because of Thy foes,
to still the enemy and the avenger.*

*When I look at Thy heavens, the work of Thy fingers
the moon and the stars which Thou hast established;
what is man that Thou art mindful of him,
and the son of man that Thou dost care for him?*

*Yet Thou hast made him little less than God, and dost
crown him with glory and honour.
Thou hast given him dominion over the
works of Thy hands;
Thou hast put all things under his feet,
all sheep and oxen,
and also the beasts of the field,
the birds of the air, and the fish of the sea,
whatever passes along the paths of the sea.*

*O Lord, our Lord, how majestic is Thy name in
all the earth!*

Psalm 8; A psalm of David

*The Lord is my shepherd, I shall not want;
He makes me lie down in green pastures.
He leads me beside still waters; He restores my soul.
He leads me in paths of righteousness for His name's sake.*

*Even though I walk through the valley of the
shadow of death,
I fear no evil; for Thou art with me;
Thy rod and Thy staff, they comfort me.*

*Thou preparest a table before me in the
presence of my enemies;
Thou anointest my head with oil, my cup overflows.*

*Surely goodness and mercy shall follow me all
the days of my life;
and I shall dwell in the house of the Lord for ever.*

Psalm 23

*Make a joyful noise to the Lord, all the lands!
Serve the Lord with gladness!
Come into His presence with singing!*

*Know that the Lord is God!
It is He that made us, and we are His;
We are His people, and the sheep of His pasture.*

*Enter His gates with thanksgiving,
and His courts with praise!
Give thanks to Him, bless His name!*

*For the Lord is good;
His steadfast love endures for ever,
and His faithfulness to all generations.*

Psalm 100

TIMELINE 1000BC TO 400BC

• Solomon's kingdom is divided into Israel in the north and Judah in the south. Jeroboam rules Israel, and Solomon's son Rehoboam rules Judah.

DECORATIVE FURNITURE FROM
SAMARIA, CAPITAL OF ISRAEL

1000BC

• Ahab becomes king of Israel, with Jezebel as his queen.

ELIJAH'S
CONTEST WITH THE
PROPHETS OF BAAL

900BC

• Isaiah is prophet to King Ahaz and King Hezekiah.

• Samaria falls to the invading Assyrians.

ISRAEL'S CAPITAL, SAMARIA, IS CAPTURED,
AND IS OCCUPIED BY THE ASSYRIANS

800BC

The Trials of Job

THE Book of Job tells the story of a rich man called Job, who was faithful to God and blessed by him. One day, a member of God's heavenly council suggests that Job's faith should be tested. He makes a bet with God that if Job were to suffer great misfortune, he would lose his faith. To find out if he is right, God gives permission for Job to be robbed of his wealth, his ten children and his health. Job's family and friends assume that his misfortunes are God's punishment for some terrible sin, and throw him out of the town.

As Job sits outside the city gates, three of his friends (known as Job's comforters) come to console him. After seven days of silence, Job pours out his feelings in a bitter lamentation and there follows a long, heated discussion about the reason for his plight which forms most of the book. Although his friends' lack of understanding drives Job to distraction, it also turns him to God. Despite his suffering, he refuses to curse God and continues to pray to Him. In the end, Job's prayers are answered. He is made twice as wealthy as he was before, he is cured of his disease, he has ten more children and goes on to live a long and happy life.

The book of Job has been called "one of the most original works in the poetry of humankind". It deals with human experience in general and, in particular, with suffering. Although in the end Job's misfortunes disappear, the story seems to contradict the basic principle that those who have faith in God will have good fortune, and people that do not will suffer. The question Job keeps asking is why God is treating him in this way. One suggestion is that Job needed to realize that he did not know everything about God, and that he could not predict God's actions. By the end of the story, Job has understood that God's wisdom and greatness are such that no human can ever fully grasp them. Job's mistake was that his idea of God was too small. When he realizes the greatness of God, his problems disappear.

Discussing the problem of suffering
This picture shows Job with his three comforters. The phrase "a Job's comforter" has come to mean a person who makes a situation worse, while apparently trying to give comfort.

• King Josiah restores the worship of God to Judah while they are occupied by the Assyrians.

• Jerusalem is captured by the Babylonians, and the Exile begins as the Jews are taken to Babylon.

KING JEHOIAKIM BURNS BARUCH'S SCROLLS

700BC

• With God's guidance, Daniel rises to a position of power in Babylon, and he is saved from the lions in the pit.

FRAGMENT FROM THE BOOK OF DANIEL

• Ezekiel brings the Jews together into a nation, worshipping God.

EZEKIEL TEACHING

600BC

• Under the guidance of God the Jews re-establish themselves in the Promised Land.

JEWS CELEBRATE COMPLETING THE NEW TEMPLE

500BC

400BC

Glossary

Baal
Baal is the main god of the Canaanites, the original inhabitants of the Promised Land. He was a fertility god, the people believed that he made the crops grow for them. He was also a thunder god, and he is often pictured holding or throwing a bolt of lightning.

Commandments
The Ten Commandments were the most important of the laws that God gave to Moses on Mount Sinai. They are addressed to the whole of the Israelite nation, and to everyone as an individual. They were the terms of the covenant between God and his people and were produced on two stone tablets. The tablets were kept in the Ark of the Covenant.

covenant
A promise where God enters into a special relationship with His people. He promised His protection and the land of Canaan to Abraham and his descendants if they would be faithful to him. This idea is summed up by the prophet Jeremiah; "I will be their God, and they will be my people." The main covenants in the Old Testament are with Abraham and Moses. In the New Testament, the main covenant is with all God's people, sealed with the death of Jesus on the cross.

Exile
This is a very important period in Jewish history. When Israel and Judah were conquered, the Israelites living there were sent from the Promised Land to live in Babylon. It was while they were living in exile that prophets such as Ezekiel were able to bring the nation together to worship God properly.

Exodus
This is the name given to the journey that the Israelites made from Egypt to the promised land. "Exodus" itself means "going out", which describes how the Israelites left Egypt.

faith
A complete trust and unquestioning belief in something or someone. Followers of God are devoted in such a way that they will do anything that is asked of them; believing that if God has requested something then it must be right.

grace
The "grace" of God is the fact that God loves all the men and women that he created even though no one on earth is completely without sin.

idol
An idol is a statue of a person, god or animal. Idolatry is worshipping the statue, which is forbidden to the Israelites in the Ten Commandments. The Israelites often forgot or ignored this rule, and had to be reminded not to worship idols by prophets from God.

Israel
This was originally the nation that descended from Jacob, who was renamed Israel after wrestling all night with an angel by the river Jabbok. The new name, which means "he who has wrestled with the Lord", was a sign that God was still with him. To punish King Solomon for disobeying Him, God split Israel into two kingdoms. Solomon's son, Rehoboam, ruled over the southern part, called Judah, while Jeroboam ruled the northern part which kept the name Israel. Jeroboam set up a new capital for Israel at Samaria. Israel was conquered by the Assyrians, and its people sent away. The capital, Samaria, was occupied by people from other countries, who became known as Samaritans.

Jew
This was the name given to the Israelites while they were in Exile in Babylon. It was originally used to mean people from Judah, but after the Exile it came to mean people who followed the Jewish faith.

Judah
This is the southern part of the divided kingdom. To punish King Solomon for disobeying Him, God split Solomon's kingdom into two. Solomon's son, Rehoboam, ruled over the southern part, called Judah, while Jeroboam ruled the northern part which kept the name Israel. The capital of Judah was Jerusalem, the holy city of the Jewish faith. When Jerusalem was captured by the Babylonians, the people were sent into exile.

miracle
These are mighty works, performed through the power of God. Moses himself performed miracles, the most famous of which is the parting of the Red Sea. They happen not only to show God's power to people, but they also form part of God revealing Himself to His creation, humans. The most important miracle to Christianity is the resurrection of Jesus after he was crucified.

Promised Land
Abraham, the ancestor of all the Israelites was promised a large area east of the Mediterranean Sea, then called the Great Sea, for his descendants. When Moses led the Exodus from Egypt, he was leading the Israelites to claim the Promised Land.

prophet
Prophets were men or women called by God to speak for Him and to communicate His will to the people. The prophets first emerged as a group in the time of Samuel, they would offer guidance to the Israelites and warn of troubles ahead.

sacrifice
An offering made to God as a way for a man to give God something that belongs to him. Only the best can be offered to God, the first born lambs, or the best wheat. Sacrifices are not a person's attempt to earn favour from God, but a way to make peace with Him.

Index

Page numbers in **bold** refer to illustrations

A

Abednego, 42, **43**
Abraham, 41
Ahab, King **10-11**, 12, **13**, 14, 15, 16, 17, **18-19**, 24, 26, 27, 28, 31
seal of, **17**
Ahasuerus, 48, **49**
Ahaz, King, 31
Ahaziah, King, 26, 30
Amaziah, King, 31
Ammonite, 40
Amon, King, 34
Amoz, 32
Amytis, 44
angel, 14, 19, 32, **33**, 43, 51
seraph, **32**
Aphek, 16
architecture, 23
armour, **18**
coat of mail, **18**
Artaxerxes, 48
Asherah, 12, 13, 17
Ashpenaz, 42
Assyria, 24, 28, 29, 30, 31, 33, 35, 38, 39, 47, 56
Athaliah, Queen, 30

B

Baal, 10, 11, 12, 13, 15, 17, 28, 62
Babylon, **6**, 33, 36, 38, 39, 40, 41, 42, 43, 44-5, 46, 47, 48, 50, 51, 52, 53
hanging gardens of, **44**
Baruch, 36

Belshazzar, **44-5**,
Benhadad, 16, 18, 19, 25, 28,
Bethel, 10, 20, 28, 29, 35
Bible, 42
brick making, **42**
Buzi, 40

C

Cherith, brook of, **11**
Chronicles, Book of, 54
Commandments, 62
covenant, 62
Cyrus, King, 44, 46, 47, **50**

D

Damascus, 15, 16, 23, 31
Dan, 10, 28, 29, 35
Daniel, 42-3, 44, 50-51,
Book of, 42-51
Darius, King, 47, 48, **49**, 50, 51
David, King, 47
desert, 14
Dothan, 24, 25
dream, **42-3**, 44
drought, 11, 12, 13

E

Edomites, 31
Egypt, 29, 39, 40, 42, 45
seal of, **12**
Elijah, **10**, **11**, **12-13**, **14-15**, **17**, 18, 19, **20-21**, 22, 26, 27, **58**
Elisha, 15, **20-21**, **22**, **23**, 24, 25, 26, 28, 29
Enoch, 6, 58

Esther, 42, **52-5**
Book of, 52-5
Ethiopia, 33, 52
Euphrates, 29
Exile, 62
Exodus, 62
Ezekiel, **40-41**, 42, 46, **59**
Ezra, 48

F

faith, 62
Feast of Tabernacles, 47

G

Gedaliah, 40
Gehazi, 22, 23
God
forgiveness of, 17
law of, 17, **34-5**
golden calves, 10, 28, **29**, 35
grace, 62

H

Haggai, **47**
Haman, 54, **55**
Hazael, 15, 28, 29, 31
Hegai, 53
Hebrew, 10, 11, 33, 42, 56
Hezekiah, King, 32, **33**, 34
High Priest, 30, 31, 34, 36
Hilkiah, 34, 36
Hoshea, 29
Huldah, **34**

I

idol, 10, 12, 26, **35**, 41, 43, 62
Imlah, 19
India, 52
Indus, River, 45
Iran, 49
Iraq, 18, 29
Isaiah, **32**, 33, 46, **59**
Israel, 10, 11, 12, 14, 16, 17, 18, 19, 22, 23, 24, 26, 28-9, 31, 33, 36, 41, 46, 47, 48, 49, 62
tribes of, 10, 13, 47

Israelites, 12, 13, 14, 15, 23, 24, 25, 26, 28, 29, 30, 33, 40, 47, 49, 62

J

Jeconiah, 38
Jehoahaz, King, 29, 37
Jehoash, King, 29
Jehoiachin, King, 37
Jehoiada, 30, 31
Jehoiakim, King, 37, 38
Jehoshaphat, 18, 19
Jehu, King, 15, **26-7**, **28**, 30
Jeremiah, **36-7**, 38, 39, 40, 41, 46, **59**
Jericho, 20, 21, 22
Jeroboam, King, 10, 28, 29
Jerusalem, 10, 29, 30, 31, 32, 33, 34, 36, 37, 38, 39, 40, 45, 46, 47, 48-9, 51
Jeshua, 47
Jewellery, **53**
Jews, 40-41, 42, 45, 46, 47, 48, 52, **54-5**, 56, 57, 62
exile of, 40-41
return from exile, 46-7
Jezebel, **10**, 11, 12, 14, 17, 26, **27**, 30
Jezreel, 13, 26, 27
Joash, King, 30-31
Job, Book of, 61
Jonah, **56-7**
Joppa, 57
Joram, King, 25, 26, 27, 28
Jordan, River, **20**, 21, **23**, 29, 39
Joshua, 40
Josiah, King, **34-5**, 37
Judah, 10, 14, 18, 26, 27, 30-31, 32, 33, 35, 36, 38-9, 40, 49, 50, 62
Judaism, 41

K

Keilah, 33
Kenite, 22, 23, 36
Kings, Book of, 48-57
Kiriathjearim, 13
Kish, 16, 17

L

Lahmu, **30**
leprosy, 23, 25, 28, **30,** 60
lion, **51**

M

make-up, 53
Manasseh, King, 34
Marduk, **51**
Medes, 44, 47, 48, 50, 52
Medean Empire, 51
Memphis, 42
Meshach, 42, **43**
Messiah, 32, 61
Micaiah, **19**, 37, 59
miracle, 12, 22, 33, 51, 62
Mordecai, 53, 54, 55
Moses, 10, 14, 34, 40, 46
Mount Carmel, **12**, 13, 14, 22
Mount Horeb, 10, 14, 62
Mount Sinai, 10, 15, 62

N

Naaman, **23**
Naboth, 17, 19, 26
Nebuchadnezzar, 38, 39, 40, 42-3, 44, 46
Nehemiah, 48
Nile, River, 29
Nimrud, 28, 31

Nineveh, 33, 43, 45, 46, 47, 56, 57
Nuzi, 18

O

Obadiah, 12
oil, **22**
    sacred, 26
Old Testament, **42**
Omri, King, 11, 24

P Q

pagan, 16
    gods, 10, 11, 12, 14, 28, 29, 30, 31, 32, 33, 34, **35**, 45, 56, see also idols
Pakistan, 45
Palestine, 45
Pashur, 36
Passover, 35, 47
Pazuzu, **35**
Persepolis, 49
Persia, 43, 44, 47, 48, 49, 52
Pharaoh, 39, 40
Philistines, 31
Phoenica, 10, 12
Promised Land, 10, 13, 29, 30, 31, 32, 38, 40, 41, 46, 47, 48-9, 50, 52, 53, 62
prophecy, 18, 19
prophet, 14, 16, 18-19, 20-21, 22, 23, 24, 25, 28, 31, 32, 36, 37, 38, 39, 40, 47, 56, 62
Psalms, Book of, 60

R

Rabshakeh, 33
Ramoth-gilead, 18
Rome, 43

S

sacrifice, 12, **13**, 29, 34, 35, 41, 47, 62
Samaria, 10, 11, 16, 17, 19, **24**, 25, 31, 33
Samaritan, 29, 47, 49

Samuel, 59
Sanballat, 48, 49
Sennacherib, 33
Shadrach, 42, **43**
Shalmaneser, 28, 29
Shaphat, 15
Shashgaz, 53
Shear-jashub, 32
Sheshbazzar, 46
Shunem, 22
Sidon, King of, 11
slavery, 22, 39
Solomon, King, 10, 31
    temple of, 31, 34, 39, 45, 46, 47, 48
Spain, 56
Susa, 52
Syria, 15, 16, 18, 19, 23, 24-5, 28, 29, 31
    jewellery of, **16**
    statue of, **16**

T

Tarshish, 56
Thebes, 42
Tigris, River, 29, 39

Tiglath-pileser, **31**
Tishbe, 11, 15
Tobiah, 48, 49
treasure, **31**, 33, 46, 52

U

Uzziah, King, **30**, 32

V

vision, 11

W

wilderness, 34
women, 22, 53

Z

Zarephath, 11, 15
Zechariah, 31, 47
Zedekiah, 18, 19, 37, 39
Zerubbabel, 47